Wallace Library	DUE DATE (stamped in blue) RETURN DATE (stamped in black)

HIPPOLYTUS IN DRAMA AND MYTH

HIPPOLYTUS
in Drama and Myth

The Hippolytus of Euripides
A new translation by Donald Sutherland

The Hippolytus of Drama and Myth
A study by Hazel E. Barnes

A Bison Original
University of Nebraska Press
1960

The authors wish to express their appreciation to the University of Colorado Council on Research and Creative Work, which supplied funds to aid in the preparation of the manuscript.

First printing, September, 1960
Second printing, December, 1963
Third printing, October, 1966

Contents

THE HIPPOLYTUS OF EURIPIDES

Translated by

DONALD SUTHERLAND

DRAMATIS PERSONAE

APHRODITE, *goddess of love*
ARTEMIS, *goddess of chastity, etc.*
THESEUS, *king of Athens*
PHAEDRA, *his wife*
HIPPOLYTUS, *his bastard son by an Amazon*
AN OLD NURSE, *belonging to Phaedra*
AN OLD SLAVE, *belonging to Hippolytus*
A MESSENGER
MALE CHORUS
FEMALE CHORUS

HIPPOLYTUS

*(Before the palace of Theseus at Troezen. On either side of
the door stands a statue, one of Artemis, the other of Aphrodite.
Enter the goddess* APHRODITE, *looking like her statue.)*

APHRODITE

       Great and not nameless am I among men,
love's goddess, Aphrodite, as in heaven.
Of all who dwell within this living world
and look still on the shining of the sun
between the seas which end the East and West,
those I advance who venerate my powers
but overturn those insolent toward me,
for this is ingrained even in the gods,
to be much pleased when honored by mankind.
Soon I will show the truth of what I say.
The son of Theseus by an Amazon,
bastard Hippolytus, whose guardian
schooled him in holiness, is the one man
in all this land of Troezen to declare
that I was born the very worst of gods,
spurns beds of love and will not hear of brides,
but honors Artemis as child of Zeus,
as sister of Apollo, reckoning her
the greatest of the gods, and every day
through the green forest he accompanies
that virgin huntress, with his rapid hounds
ridding the land of game, since he has found
company greater than is meant for man.
It is not this I grudge him. Why should I?
But for his slights to *me* I shall today

5

have my revenge upon Hippolytus.
Nor need I trouble much. Most of this work
I have rough-hewn already, long ago.
Once, when he ventured from his guardian's house
to visit Athens, where his father ruled,
and watch the solemn Mysteries, to be made
one of the pure, his father's noble wife,
Phaedra, beheld him and was overcome,
through my designs, by irresistible love.
Before she came here to Troezen she raised
a temple to me, on a height which looks
across the gulf to Troezen, where he was,
her absent love. Only to have his love
in time to come she offered me that shrine.
Then Theseus, to escape a taint of blood
he shed in Athens, sailed here with his wife,
agreeing to an exile of one year,
but since then, sighing, frenzied by love's goads,
his wife, poor woman, languishes away
in silence. Not one of the household slaves
knows her disease. But this love must not end
in silence. I will make the matter known
to Theseus, and it all shall be exposed.
This lad who wars against me shall be slain
by his own father's curses, which the lord
of seas, Poseidon, gave to Theseus once,
that he might call upon the god three times
and not in vain. And Phaedra, though her honor
is yet unblemished, still must also die.
For her misfortune shall not count with me
more than exacting from my enemies
punishment on the scale I owe myself.
But as I see the son of Theseus,
Hippolytus, approach, who has left off

the labor of the hunt, I shall depart.
With him there follows an attendant rout
of many servants, yelping hymns of praise
to Artemis. He does not know the gates
of death stand open for him. and the day
whose light he now looks on shall be his last.
> *(Exit. Enter* HIPPOLYTUS *with a*
> *chorus of hunters.)*

★

HIPPOLYTUS AND CHORUS
> Follow her, follow her, raising a song to her,
> Artemis, heavenly daughter of Zeus!
> Follow her, sing to her, we who belong to her!

CHORUS
> Maiden most powerful, maiden most high,
> offspring of Zeus,
> hail, all hail! On thee we cry,
> daughter of Leto and Zeus.
> Fairest of maidens, fairest far,
> dwelling far within the sky
> where the lordliest mansions are,
> where the starriest mansion is,
> where thy lord and father Zeus
> treads a glittering golden hall,
> hail, O fairest, fairest of all
> maids on Olympus, Artemis!

★

HIPPOLYTUS *(to the statue of Artemis)*
> Lady, this woven crown I bring for thee,
> of flowers I gathered in a meadowland
> where neither shepherd dare pasture his flocks

nor ploughshare ever came, but in the spring
the bee alone explores the virgin field.
Virtue itself maintains a garden there
with dews from running streams. Those men alone
who have not training but a natural gift
for temperance in all things equally
may gather there what evil men may not.
But, my dear lady, from a hallowed hand
receive this garland for thy golden hair,
for I am favored as no other man,
to be with thee and even speak with thee,
hearing thy voice, though seeing not thine eyes.
Thus may my course of life run till its end.

OLD SLAVE

Sir—not my lord, since lords we call the gods—
would you accept some kind advice from me?

HIPPOLYTUS

By all means. Otherwise I'd seem a fool.

OLD SLAVE

Well, do you know the custom among men?

HIPPOLYTUS

I don't. Not even what your question means.

OLD SLAVE

They hate the lofty and exclusive kind.

HIPPOLYTUS

They should. What proud man is endurable?

OLD SLAVE

Affable men, though, have a certain charm?

HIPPOLYTUS

Great charm; great profit, too, for such brief work.

OLD SLAVE

Do you expect it is the same with gods?

HIPPOLYTUS

Yes, if our human customs come from them.

OLD SLAVE

Then why not charm with greetings a proud god?

HIPPOLYTUS

Which god?—unless the name be dangerous.

OLD SLAVE

There—Aphrodite—standing at your door.

HIPPOLYTUS

I greet her from a distance, being chaste.

OLD SLAVE

Remember she is proud. Men honor her.

HIPPOLYTUS

One takes one's choice, of gods as of mankind.

OLD SLAVE

May you have sense to make a happy choice!

HIPPOLYTUS

I like no god whose wonders work by night.

OLD SLAVE

Take things—my boy—at the gods' estimate.

HIPPOLYTUS

Go, men, pass in and see about our food.
After the hunt full tables are a joy.
And rub the horses down, so when I'm fed
full I can yoke them to my chariot
and exercise them properly. To her,
your Aphrodite, I say fare you well!

(*Exit into the palace*)

OLD SLAVE

But we—for we should not do as the young—
thus, with the deference befitting slaves,
bow low before thine image and we pray,
our lady Aphrodite. When someone,
forced by his youth, carries his heart too high,

thou must forgive him for his reckless words.
Pretend thou not to hear them. For the gods
must have more wisdom than we mortals have.

(*Exit into the palace with the other attendants except a few who go to care for the horses R. Enter L a* CHORUS OF TROEZENIAN WOMEN, *some with jugs, some with laundry baskets, etc. A few, one carrying a basket of purple clothing, go into the palace. The remaining chorus may be composed of five women, of differing voices, ages, and characters. 1 is a lead soprano, 2 an alto, 3 a young wife, mezzo soprano or alto, 4 a contralto and not young, 5 a girlish soprano.*)

★★

CHORUS

1.   Sprung from the deep, they say, dripping,   *Strophe a*
        a stream descends a rock that flings
        forth from its crests for the dipping
        of pitchers the foaming of springs.
        There my friend had rinsed and wrung
        the royal mantles of purple in dews
        tossed by the downpour of water and flung
        them one by one
        wide on the rock's back warm in the sun.
        She herself told me the news

        first, that our lady is ailing   *Antistrophe a'*
        and hides inside the house in bed,
        shadowy draperies veiling
        the glimmering blond of her head.
        Now three days I hear have passed:
        the Queen has taken no morsel of bread
        into her lips, as if meaning to fast
        and hide her pain
        still, till she anchor out of the main,
        safe in the port of the dead.

2. Is your spirit possessed by Pan,   *Strophe b*
   young woman, or Hecate's spell,
   or by Corybant revel,
   or may Cybele the mountain
   mother impel you to wander?

3. Or did you fail to fulfill
   some offering owed to Artemis when you still
   dwelt in Crete and offend her?
   She follows by land or by sea
   on loud whirling of waves lightly.

4. May your husband, so nobly born   *Antistrophe b'*
   and leader of Athens, be led
   round at home by some slave's bed
   and yours be secretly forlorn?

5. Could there have entered our waters,
   free to all craft and all crews,
   some mariner bound from Crete with disastrous
       news?
   Grief so sudden it shatters
   the soul may have driven the Queen
   to bed, binding her there, stricken.

4. The recalcitrant nerves of woman are prone   (c)
   often to such dire
   uncontrollable despair, most often if one
   be pregnant or reckless under desire.

3. Yet one time when that impulse breathed in my
       womb   *(c')*
   "Artemis!" I cried,
   "Queen of arrows, of birth-pangs, come now to my
       side!"
   and always, when I have prayed, she has come.

5. But here the old nurse comes with her now,   **(d)**
    bearing her up when she falters,
    a darkening cloud of gloom on her brow.
    I wonder, what can it have been?
    What is it alters
    the color and force of the Queen?

(PHAEDRA *stays at the door, unwilling to come further out.* MAIDS
bring out a couch, coverlets, a sunhat with veils, etc. PHAEDRA
turns back toward the interior of the palace. The NURSE *is a
soprano, but harder and harsher and older than #5—singing* d'
in the same register as d, *but with immense textural difference.*)

NURSE

Oh ills and cruel diseases of men!   **(d')**
Always afflicted or pining!
And what am I to do for you, then?
Or what am I not to do? There,
there is your shining
of sunlight, and there is your air!
And there, outdoors at last, is your bed!   **(d'')**
Coming out here's what you wanted.
You talked of nothing else. And instead
you'll suddenly want to go back,
bored, discontented,
in love with whatever you lack,
with all that you have, disenchanted.
                              (*to* CHORUS)

(*declaimed*)

Better be sick than be a nurse.
The one is simple, the other has
anguish of intellect, and worse,
hard labor. But laborious
is man's whole life. We have no rest.
And what might be more to our taste

than life, the darkness holds embraced
and hides in shadow. It is plain
we are not lucky in our love
of life, when what is here above
seems bright because we cannot gain
experience of a life below:
by myths we're carried to and fro.

PHAEDRA (*contralto*)
Raise up my body, lift my head.
All my limbs, my friends, are weak.
Girls, hold these arms, so white, so sleek.
This hat is far too heavy to wear.
Off! Ringlets down my shoulders spread.

NURSE
Be brave, my dear! Don't roughly toss
your body here and there.
Only be calm and brace your mind
with noble purpose. You will find
your illness easier to bear.
Trouble must come to all of us.

PHAEDRA (*singing but not full voice*)
Ah! ah!
If only I might drink my fill
out of some dewy little spring
of virgin waters and lie still
under poplars in the deep
grasses of a field to sleep!

NURSE
My child, what is this clamoring?
You must not cry such things aloud
nor fling such thoughts before a crowd
as winds of madness raise in you!

PHAEDRA (*full voice*)
Oh take me to the hills! I go

up to the woods, along the pines
where fanged and killing hounds race through
to circle round the dappled roe!
Oh gods! how I desire to hear
their baying, and to shout, to hold
the javelin balanced next my ear,
against my floating hair that shines
like yellow gold,
a bladed shaft in hand!

NURSE (*accompanied or half-sung*)

What in the world has made you think,
my child, of those things? What concern
have you with hunts and hounds at all?
Whatever is it makes you yearn
for running springs, when near the wall
an incline of the watered land
gathers a stream where you may drink?

PHAEDRA (*fullest voice*)

O goddess of our sweeping shores
near Limna, where the foaming speed
of surf and racing horses roars,
O Artemis, along that plain
if I might ride and break and train
colts of the prompt Venetian breed!

NURSE (*half-sung as before*)

What is it now? Your spirit raves.
Just now, my child, you climbed a hill
where longing sent you after game
but now you only long to tame
colts on the sands above the waves.
Such things require no little skill
of any prophet who would say
what god draws up the reins so tight
and whips your spirit from the right

track so, making it bolt away.

PHAEDRA

Alas! Whatever have I done?
Where have I wandered from my mind?
Some power destroys me, I have run
mad! I am lost! My veils, Nurse, wind
once more about me, hide my head!
At those wild words I think I said
I am ashamed. Oh hide me! Tears
fall from these eyes which do not know
which way to turn for shame. What pain,
coming to one's right mind again!
Even madness does not torture so,
for it destroys one unawares.

NURSE *(declaimed)*

I hide you, so. When will death hide
my body ever? Oh,
much life has taught me much. I know
that mortal man should never drink
the wine of sympathy unmixed
nor drench the marrow of his mind.
Affection should be loosely fixed
so one may have it tightly tied
or else unbind.
It's hard when one soul aches for two,
as now I feel her pain with her.
Yet life too closely planned, some think,
makes one more vexed, not happier,
and interferes with health. How true!
So that I find I think much less
of any good's extremity
than of that "nothing to excess"—
and wise men will agree with me.

★

FIRST MEMBER OF CHORUS

>   Old woman, our Queen Phaedra's trusted nurse,
>   we see the pitiable state she's in,
>   but have no way of telling what is wrong,
>   so we should like to hear of it from you.

NURSE

>   I do not know. I ask, but she won't say.

FIRST MEMBER OF CHORUS

>   Not even how her sufferings began?

NURSE

>   No use. She will not breathe a word of it.

FIRST MEMBER OF CHORUS

>   How weak her body seems and worn away!

NURSE

>   Of course. She has been three days without food.

FIRST MEMBER OF CHORUS

>   Because of madness, or a will to die?

NURSE

>   To die. She fasts to get away from life.

FIRST MEMBER OF CHORUS

>   How can her husband be content with this?

NURSE

>   She hides her suffering and denies she's ill.

FIRST MEMBER OF CHORUS

>   But can't he tell by looking at her face?

NURSE

>   He happens to be out of Troezen now.

FIRST MEMBER OF CHORUS

>   Why don't you force her then, and try to find
>   what her disease is, what affects her mind?

NURSE

>   I have tried everything and done no good.
>   But I don't give up trying even now.
>   See for yourself, so you can testify

what sort I show I am when trouble comes
upon my masters. Come now, my dear child:
let's both forget the things we said before
and you be sweeter now, relax that sad
and scowling brow, that deviating mind—
and I, though then I wrongly followed you
so both of us were lost, I give it up
and set out for another, better, course.
Now if your malady is one of those
one does not mention, there are women here
who might confer and find you some relief.
Or, if your trouble's of another kind
and need not be concealed in front of men,
speak out, and let the doctors know what's wrong.
Oh, very well, then! Why be silent? Child,
you should not be so silent, but at least
correct me if I speak improperly
or else agree when what I say is right.
Say *some*thing! Here, look at me. Woe is me!
Women, these efforts are a waste of time:
we stand exactly where we did before.
My words made no impression on her then
nor will she listen now. (*to* PHAEDRA) But know **one**
    thing—
and in the face of *this* be more self-willed
than is the open sea: if you should die
and so betray your sons, who will not share
their father's wealth—no! that hard-riding queen
the Amazon, who gave birth to a lord
for sons of yours—a bastard, but who keeps
nobility in view—you know him well,
Hippolytus—

PHAEDRA

No no!

NURSE

That touches you?

PHAEDRA

It kills me, Nurse. Henceforth, about that man,
I beg you, by the gods, to say no more.

NURSE

You see? Your mind is clear, and yet you lack
the will to help your sons and stay alive.

PHAEDRA

I love my children, but Fortune has raised
another storm of dangers, where I drown.

NURSE

But *you* have kept your hands quite pure of blood?

PHAEDRA

My hands are pure; my mind, though, has a stain.

NURSE

But no foe from outside has done you harm?

PHAEDRA

A friend has, willing it no more than I.

NURSE

Has Theseus done you wrong in any way?

PHAEDRA

Rather, let him not find that *I* fail *him*.

NURSE

What drives you, then, to fail him by your death?

PHAEDRA

Let me do wrong. It is not you I wrong.

NURSE

I dare not. Your fault will be laid to me.

PHAEDRA

Take care! You hurt my hand, clinging so hard!

NURSE

And to your knees, and never shall let go.

PHAEDRA

    Poor Nurse, woe to you if you learn my woes!

NURSE

    What could be worse for me than losing you?

PHAEDRA

    You'll die for it. Yet honor shall be mine.

NURSE

    Then why refuse to tell me, if it's good?

PHAEDRA

    It's base, though I'll make excellence of it.

NURSE

    Would you not be more honored, if you told?

PHAEDRA

    Oh, for the gods' sake, go; let go my hand!

NURSE

    Not till you give to me the gift you owe.

PHAEDRA

    Yes, for I honor your devoted hand.

NURSE

    Let me be still now. It's your turn to speak.

PHAEDRA

    O desperate mother, what a love you loved!

NURSE

    You mean the bull, child? Or what do you mean?

PHAEDRA

    And you, bold sister, Dionysus' bride!

NURSE

    My child, what's wrong? Why speak ill of your kin?

PHAEDRA

    And I the third, ruined how pitiably!

NURSE

    You frighten me. What is this leading to?

PHAEDRA

    To our sad destiny, no recent thing.

NURSE

> I still know nothing that I want to hear.

PHAEDRA

> If only you could say what I must say.

NURSE

> I am no prophet, seeing in the dark.

PHAEDRA

> What is it—what they say men do—to love?

NURSE

> Both very sweet, my child, and painful, too.

PHAEDRA

> Yes. I have come to know the latter well.

NURSE

> What's that? You are in love, my child? With whom?

PHAEDRA

> What do you call him—oh, the Amazon's—

NURSE

> You say Hippolytus?

PHAEDRA

> You say, not I.

NURSE

> Alas, what *will* you say! Oh, now indeed
> you take my life! O friends, can you bear this?
> I shall not bear it, living! I loathe this day,
> this daylight! Oh I shall cast off and quit
> this body, and exchange this life for death!
> Farewell! I am no more. For virtue loves—
> although against its will—loves wickedness.
> This Aphrodite is no god at all,
> but surely something greater than a god,
> who has destroyed her, and me, and this house!

★ ★ ★ ★

CHORUS

1. Ah did you hear

2. Oh did you heed

1. what we never should hear,
   the pitiful plaint and wail of the Queen?

4. Oh may I perish before I meet
   despair like yours, my dear, my dear!

3. & 5. Poor woman, poor woman, to have such pain!

2, 3, 4. Ah woes that feed
   mankind like wheat,
   our daily food!

2. & 3. Oh your ruin is plain! Ah your trouble is known!

1,2,3,4,5 What will the rest of this long day bring?

3. The palace will soon see done
   some new strange thing.

1. Ah now we have seen,
   we have understood,
   how Aphrodite's enchantment may ravage one!

1. & 2. O unfortunate daughter of Crete!

★

PHAEDRA

Women of Troezen, who inhabit here
the outermost approach of Pelops' isle,
in the long hours of night I have not slept
for wondering why the life of man goes bad.
I think that not according to their gifts
of mind do they decline, since many are wise,
but one should see it this way: we all know
the good and see it plain, but will not work
to have it, some from indolence, and some

prefer some other pleasure than the one
of honor. And life's pleasures are not few,
like long discussions, leisure, a sweet vice,
and love.* There are two loves, the one not bad,
the other a disaster to the house.
But if the case were clear, this double thing
would not be written with a single name.
So then, since I had long been of this mind,
no kind of drug or philtre could corrupt
or make me see the question otherwise.
I shall confide to you my train of thought:
when first I felt love's wound I tried to see
how best I might endure it, and began
by silence and concealing the disease.
The tongue's not to be trusted. Though it does
know how to discipline the wayward thoughts
of others, it yet keeps a jealous guard
on its own many evils. Secondly,
I was determined to wear out and quell
this mindless passion by my continence.
And thirdly, when I still did not succeed
in mastering Aphrodite, then I chose
to die—who will deny it?—the best plan.
I would not have the good I do unknown
nor many witnesses if I do ill.
I knew the sick desire is a disgrace
as is the deed itself. Besides I knew
too well I was a woman, and must be
abhorred by all. Perish her very name,
who first defiled her bed with other men.
And out of noble houses this ill first
grew among women. When nobility

---

*In the original, an untranslatable distinction between *aidos* (honor) and *aidos* (shame).

prefers base action, then indeed the base
will think it noble. Women who in words
are chaste but secretly possess a wild
audacity of shamelessness, I hate.
O Aphrodite, lady of the seas,
how can they look their husbands in the face,
not shudder lest their own accomplice, night,
or their own rooms should ever find a voice?
And that, friends, is the reason why I die—
never to be found out bringing disgrace
upon my husband nor upon the sons
I bore to him, that they may live free men,
outspoken, prospering, honored for my sake,
in glorious Athens. For it will debase,
make slavish even an intrepid heart,
to know his mother's or his father's crimes.
Whatever his rank, they say that he alone
can long contend with life who has a mind
noble and honest. Time does not forbear
to hold the mirror close, close as one might
to a young girl, and shows the wicked plain.
May no one ever see me in their place!

FIRST MEMBER OF CHORUS

Ah yes! Virtue is far and near most fair
and yields a fruit of good fame upon earth.

NURSE

My lady, learning what your trouble is
gave me just now a dreadful sudden fright;
I see now I was foolish. Second thoughts
somehow are wiser thoughts in mortal heads.
You suffer nothing rare nor beyond reach
of reason. And a god inspired these pangs.
You love. What's strange in that? Most mortals do.
And then, because of love to take your life!

They surely stand to lose who fall in love—
or are about to fall—if die they must.
True, Aphrodite cannot be withstood
when in full violence she storms the heart—
she who comes quietly on one who yields
but, if she find him insolent and proud,
seizes and drags him down, outrages him
beyond belief. She journeys through the air,
and even in the billows of the sea
is Aphrodite, and all things are born
of her. It's she who sows the seed and gives
the love from which all we on earth are sprung.
And so those men who keep the written lore
of ancient times and always live themselves
with goddesses, the Muses, know it well,
how Zeus once fell in love with Semele,
and how the shining goddess of the dawn
snatched Cephalus away up to the gods,
for love of him. Yet *they* stay on in heaven
and never try to break free from their gods,
having grown fond of being overcome,
I daresay, by misfortune of this kind.
But you will not endure it? Then your sire
should have begotten you on other terms
and under other gods than those we have,
if you will not accept these easy ways.
How many men of good sense, do you think,
seeing their beds corrupted, *will* not see?
How many fathers, when their sons get wild,
arrange their loves for them? For wise men find
mortals do well to keep their failings hid.
Nor should a man work too hard at his life:
the covered beams in your own roof are not
squared to perfection. Fallen as you are

into such seas of Fortune, do you think
you can swim clear of them? No, you'll do well,
being but mortal woman, if you have
more good than evil. But, O my dear child,
leave off your wicked thoughts, leave off your pride,
since it is nothing but excessive pride,
this wish to be superior to the gods.
Be brave—as a god wills it—brave in love.
Take illness easy and you'll master it.
And there are charms to sing and spoken spells—
a drug of some kind will occur to us.
Men would be late with their discoveries
unless we women found a trick or two.

FIRST MEMBER OF CHORUS

Phaedra, though what she says is of more use
against this trouble, I approve you more.
Yet this praise must be more inopportune
than what she says, more harsh for you to hear.

PHAEDRA

This is what ruins great cities of the world,
not only homes, these too fine arguments.
One should not say things to delight the ears
but something whereby honor may be gained.

NURSE

Why will you talk such bombast? What you need
is not fine-figured language, but the man!
We must at once investigate the truth,
speaking aloud the straight account of you.
Don't think that if your life were not at stake
or if your nature were more temperate
I ever would have brought you down to this,
just for your pleasure with a man in bed.
No, now I fight against you to preserve
your life, and no one can find fault with that!

PHAEDRA

> To say such dreadful things! Lock up your mouth!
> Never again let slip such shameless talk!

NURSE

> Shameless, but better than fine words for you.
> Better the deed, too, if it save your life,
> than a mere name, to boast of which you die.

PHAEDRA

> Oh, by the gods!—for you speak evil well—
> go not beyond this much! I have endured
> to lose my life to love, and that is well,
> but if you plead for evil handsomely,
> I shall be utterly destroyed, reduced
> to that dishonor which I now escape.

NURSE

> With such opinions, you should not have swerved!
> But even so, obey me: graciousness
> comes next to virtue. Somewhere in the house
> are philtres and allaying balms for love—
> I just now thought of them—which will arrest
> the course of your disorder, at no risk
> of shame or any damage to the mind,
> so long as you are patient and behave.
> Then we must take some token of the man
> you now desire, some writing or some shred
> cut from his cloak, to join two charms in one.

PHAEDRA

> But is the drug an ointment or a draught?

NURSE

> I don't know. You need help, not knowledge, child.

PHAEDRA

> I fear lest I may find you far too wise.

NURSE

> Then anything might scare you! What's this dread?

PHAEDRA

That you let Theseus' son learn any of this.

NURSE

Leave that to me. I shall arrange this well.
Only, O Aphrodite of the seas,
be thou my helper! And such other things
as I intend to do I shall not need
to tell to anyone but friends inside.
    (*Exit*)

CHORUS

✦ ✦

Ah Love, ah Love, from whose eyes distill   (*a*)
the lights of desire, who cast a charm
of sweetness on those you move to kill,
Oh visit me never, bringing harm,
nor out of time, out of key!
Meteors, lightning-blasts
burn not so overwhelmingly
as Aphrodite's dazzling brand
which Love so lightly casts
from a delicate hand.

In vain, in vain does the land of Greece   (*a'*)
in Delphic Apollo's holiest hall
our slaughter of oxen still increase
while offering none to Love at all,
though well we know Love, who is
despot of gods, of men,
who keeps the dear and secret keys
to Aphrodite's inmost rooms,
but woe to mortals when
on his conquests he comes!

Once Oechalia's pride,   (b)
a filly unbroken to bed,
unridden by men and unwed,
Iole was broken at last.
The palace trembled and shook at her tread
when Aphrodite drove her fast
as Bacchantes can reel or a Naiad can run,
through blood, through smoke, to be a bride
veiled in murder, given away
to Heracles, Alcmena's son.
Oh pitiful girl, for your wedding day!

Thebes' miraculous wall!   (b′)
O murmuring mouth of the fount
of Dirce! You both could recount
how swift Aphrodite may move,
for twin-flamed thunder and lightning enwound
the bridal bed of Zeus's love
who bore the twice-born Dionysus in death.
And Aphrodite willed it all:
over all things equally
she breathes a deadly honeyed breath
and moves in her flight like some honeybee.

✶

PHAEDRA
    Be silent, women! Ah, my end has come!
FIRST MEMBER OF CHORUS
    What horror is it, Phaedra, in your house?
PHAEDRA
    Be still! I catch their voices from inside.
FIRST MEMBER OF CHORUS
    I will be still. This prelude bodes no good.
PHAEDRA
    Ah me! Ay ay! Ay ay!
    Alas for me and where my passions lead!

CHORUS

1. What is the moan you cried?

2. What is the word you wail?

3. What do you hear, O Phaedra, that makes you quail,

2. & 3. stricken and terrified?

PHAEDRA

I am lost utterly. Stand by these doors.
Hear what a tumult rages in the house.

CHORUS

3. *You* are close to the door.

4. If word comes from your house, it is you it is for.

5. But what evil has happened?

3. & 5. Tell, tell it to us!

PHAEDRA

The son of that horse-fancying Amazon
is shouting, bawling outrage at my nurse.

CHORUS

2. Yes, I do hear the noise, but I cannot make out
any words of the voice.

4. They must come through the doors to you plain in that
shout.

PHAEDRA

There, all too plainly he calls her aloud
a foul bawd who betrays her master's bed.

CHORUS

4. *You* are betrayed!

2. That's true!

3. Yes, and betrayed by a friend!

    5. All of your secrets out!

1. & 2. So it *is* the end!

2, 3, 4. How shall we counsel you?

PHAEDRA

    Ah me! No end of woes!
    Telling my troubles she has ruined me,
    meaning to cure them, if by evil means.

FIRST MEMBER OF CHORUS

    But what will you do now, trapped as you are?

PHAEDRA

    I only know one thing—to die at once,
    the only cure for my afflictions now.

(HIPPOLYTUS *comes bursting out, followed by the* NURSE. *He does not see* PHAEDRA, *who remains by the door behind him.*)

HIPPOLYTUS

    O mother Earth! O flowerings of the light!
    Oh what forbidden speech my ears have heard!

NURSE

    Someone will hear your shouts. Be still, my son.

HIPPOLYTUS

    I cannot, having heard such terrible things!

NURSE

    Be still, I beg, by this fine arm of yours!

HIPPOLYTUS

    Keep your hands off! And do not touch my cloak!

NURSE

    Oh, by your knees! Oh do not get me killed!

HIPPOLYTUS

    How?—if, as you say, you said nothing wrong?

NURSE

    This story, child, is not for everyone.

HIPPOLYTUS

    Are not good things the better when divulged?

NURSE

My son, do not dishonor your own vows.

HIPPOLYTUS

My tongue swore, but my mind remains unsworn.

NURSE

What will you do, child? Not destroy your friends!

HIPPOLYTUS (*spits*)

You soil the word! I have no wicked friends.

NURSE

Forgive, forgive! To err is human, child!

HIPPOLYTUS

O Zeus, why have you sent this counterfeit,
this vileness, Woman, to inhabit the world?
For if you meant to seed the human race,
not out of women should it be supplied,
but each man in your temples paying out
some weight of gold, or silver, or of bronze,
to buy the seed for offspring. And each man
would get his money's worth, and live at home
with no females about, in liberty.

(*to the audience*)

But now, bringing this pest into our homes,
we first lay out our fortune, like a corpse;
this proves how great an evil a wife is:
her father, who begot and brought her up,
banishes her and pays a dowry too,
to get rid of the monster. And the man
who takes the noxious growth into his house
is glad to cover up with handsome jewels
so miserable an idol, and improve
its shape with draperies as best he can—
poor fellow, sapping his economy.
And he is forced, if he has got himself
fine in-laws, to be happy lest he lose

her bitter bed, or, if he gets a bed
that serves his turn, but worthless relatives,
he downs his ills by doting on his good.
His yoke sits easiest whose wife is null,
but out of sheer simplicity of mind
stays fast at home, untouched by enterprise.
I loathe a clever woman. In my house
let there not be one more intelligent
than women should be. Aphrodite breeds
a lot more mischief in the clever ones,
who stop at nothing, but the helpless kind
have too few brains to make fools of themselves.
No servant ever should have been allowed
near to a wife; rather some voiceless kind
of beast with teeth should keep wives company,
so that they could not speak to anyone,
nor get back any messages by them.
Now bad wives can accomplish their bad schemes
indoors, with maids to do their part outside.
      (*to* NURSE)
Just as you now, you walking infamy,
have come to me, proposing intercourse
in an untouchable, a sacred bed,
my father's! I shall wipe away those words
with fresh and living waters, splashing them
into my ears. How could I be that foul,
when even having heard such things I feel
impure? It is my piety alone
that saves you, woman, understand that well,
for had I not been taken off my guard,
tricked into swearing silence by the gods,
I'd never keep myself from telling this,
all, to my father. Now, I leave this house
so long as Theseus is away from home,

and though I'll keep my mouth shut, I'll return
when *he* does, to observe you facing him,
you and your mistress, both. I'll relish that,
for I'll appreciate how bold you are.
> (*to* CHORUS)

Curse all of you! I'll never have enough
of hating women!—even if I'm told
I never change my theme. Neither do they,
but always manage somehow to be vile.
> (*to audience, taking* A CHORIST *by the throat*)

Either let someone show me they are chaste
or let me trample on these creatures still.
> (*casts* CHORIST *off and exit.*)

★

CHORUS
(Music from CHORUS—"Ah did you hear")

1. Hopeless indeed,
2. luckless and hard,
1. is the lot of our sex!
   What skill do we have, what cause can we plead
4. so as to slacken the guilt that his
   arraignment fastens round our necks?

PHAEDRA

I have what we richly deserve, in this!
O Earth! O Sun!
I know not how
to find a way
of escape from these toils
or to hide what I've done!
Which of the gods would defend me, say?
What mortal would share my place,
admitting a share in my
iniquities?

The crime, the disgrace
that comes on me now
is insurmountable, deadly unless one die.
Ah most wretched of women am I!

★

FIRST MEMBER OF CHORUS

Alas, your maid's devices went awry,
my lady, and there is no mending them.

PHAEDRA

O vilest of all women! O you base
destroyer of your friends! See how you have
undone me! May my father Zeus with fire
scar you, uproot you, grind you from the world!
Did I not say—foreseeing what you meant—
to speak no word about those things which now
I am reviled for? You could not keep still,
and so I cannot die with honor now.
But now I need some new account of this,
because that boy whose mind is whetted sharp
with wrath will tell his father of your crimes,
calling them mine. He'll tell old Pittheus,
who trained him to such virtue, what befell,
fill the whole country with the scandalous tale.
Curse you, and all who are so eager to do
their friends such ruinous good against their will.

NURSE

You can reproach me for the harm I've done,
my lady, for stinging regret controls
your judgment. Yet I too could say something
to answer this, if you would hear me out.
I brought you up. I wish you well. I tried
to find a medicine for your disease
but found not what I wanted. If I had,
had I succeeded, now I would be ranked

among the sages. For intelligence
is ours, or not, depending on our luck.

PHAEDRA

And so you make things right! And I must be
quite satisfied when, after stabbing me,
you have the goodness to agree you did!

NURSE

Let us be briefer. I was indiscreet.
But we can yet be saved from this, my child.

PHAEDRA

Stop talking! You advised me before this
not at all well, and what you did you did
badly. But go now. Get out of the way.
Look to yourself. And as for my concerns,
I shall arrange them very well myself.

(*The* NURSE *pulls her shawl over her head and begins to go away
from the palace.*)

And you, O well-born daughters of Troezen,
I beg of you to grant me just this much:
to hide in silence all you have heard here.

(*Exit* NURSE *R.*)

CHORUS

I swear by sacred Artemis, the child
of highest Zeus, I never shall expose
any of your misfortunes to the light.

PHAEDRA

Well said. Having considered everything,
I find one cure for this calamity,
one only, which can still assure my sons
an honorable life and even bring
some good to me, as things have turned out now,
for I shall never, clinging to my one life,
bring shame upon the palaces of Crete,
nor, charged with these foul deeds, meet Theseus' eyes.

FIRST MEMBER OF CHORUS
> Then you do plan an action past recall?

PHAEDRA
> To die. Just how, I shall decide myself.

FIRST MEMBER OF CHORUS
> Be careful what you say! The gods—

PHAEDRA
> Oh yes,
> you too by all means give me good advice!
> But I shall give great pleasure to the god
> who does destroy me, Aphrodite, soon,
> when I give up my life to her today,
> for I have lost out to a bitter love.
> Yet I shall be disaster when I die,
> for someone else, till he knows how to curb
> that arrogant contempt of what I feel.
> In this disorder he shall have a share
> with me, and learn how to control himself.
>
>   (*Exit into palace*)

★

CHORUS
Oh might I be in the deepest caves   (*a*)
under the world, or might I change
into a bird, and a god give wings,
send me to dwell
among the droves of flying things,
to soar and range
above the Adriatic waves,
along the sunset shore that hears
the waters of the Po come in,
where, into the seething crimson swell
thrice-mournful poplars which have been
the daughters of the setting sun,

sorrowing still for Phaethon,
shed stars of glowing amber tears.

Oh might I come where unwearyingly   **(a')**
sing the remote Hesperides,
guarding the apples of gleaming gold,
where from our eyes
and sails at last the gods withhold
the marbled seas,
and set the limit of the sky
which Atlas bears; where fountains rise,
ambrosial fountains rise and fall,
near Zeus's unweathered palaces,
near where he sleeps, the lord of all;
where far diviner ground than ours
yields to the gods more fruits, more flowers,
and ever more felicities.

O white-winged ship! oh how did you dare   **(b)**
fly from Crete through the crashing foam
of the rough salt sea conveying my queen
from her affluent home,
when the gain has been
a ruinous wedding, a desperate bride?
Oh a bird of ill omen to either side
was the ship when it flew from the land of Crete
to glorious Athens and anchored there,
when they made the ends of the hawsers fast
on Munichium's beach and the crew at last
felt the sands of the mainland under their feet!

All signs for her!—foretelling a life   **(b')**
Aphrodite might overwhelm
with unholy passion's terrible gales,
which have shattered her helm
and her brilliant sails,

and high from the rafters she knew as a bride
she will fasten a rope now, securely tied
round her delicate throat, in abhorrence of
that pow'r of the seas whose malignant strife
she will change at last for immortal fame,
to abide with honor, escaping shame,
all the tempest of mind, the torment of love!

*(Here the play can be broken for an intermission. When the
curtain rises again, a or á can be sung again.)*

VOICES OF MAIDS INSIDE

Help!　Help!
Come help, O anybody near the house!
Our lady, Theseus' wife, hangs in a noose!

CHORUS

It's done!　The queenly woman is no more!
Alas, held fast now by the rope she hung!

VOICES OF MAIDS INSIDE

Hurry!　Oh someone bring steel-bladed shears
so we can cut this knot loose from her neck!

SEMICHORUS

What shall we do, friends?　Should we go inside
and free our lady from the strangling rope?

SEMICHORUS

Why?　Her young maids are there inside with her.
To interfere now is to risk our lives.

VOICES OF MAIDS INSIDE

Straighten her limbs, stretch the poor body out.
this is the bitterest chore our lords impose.
　　　(Enter THESEUS*)*

FIRST MEMBER OF CHORUS

From what I hear now, the poor woman's dead.
Already they are laying out her corpse.

THESEUS

> Women, what was that shouting in the house?
> Does any of you know? A heavy cry
> of womenservants reached me. And the house
> does not see fit to open its doors wide
> and greet me gladly upon my return
> from consultation with the oracle.
> Is it some news about old Pittheus?
> He is well on in life, but even so,
> if he should leave us, all our house would grieve.

FIRST MEMBER OF CHORUS

> This happening, Theseus, has not touched the old.
> It is the young have died and bring you pain.

THESEUS

> Ah! Is a child of mine bereft of life?

FIRST MEMBER OF CHORUS

> Your children live. Their mother, sir, is dead.

THESEUS

> You say—my wife is dead? How did she die?

FIRST MEMBER OF CHORUS

> She tied a hanging noose around her neck.

THESEUS

> Frozen by grief or driven by some wrong?

FIRST MEMBER OF CHORUS

> That's all we know. For we too have just come,
> Theseus, in time to share your grief with you.

THESEUS

> Alas, why do I wear about my head
> this crown of woven leaves, when I receive
> this angry answer from the oracle?
> Loosen the bars, servants, open these gates!
> Unlock! that I may see the bitter sight
> of her, my wife, who, dying, ruined me.

(The doors open, disclosing the body of PHAEDRA, *with a* HAND-
MAID *or so.)*

CHORUS

Oh oh, poor woman! Ay ay!
Oh pitiful plight!
to have dealt and endured
a blow so great it brings this palace down!
Oh oh your daring! with violent might
in that unholy passion to die,
by yourself outwrestled and overthrown
in the grip of that pitiful hand!
Who was it fanned
such fires and has your life obscured?

★

THESEUS

Alas, my many labors; My people, this
is far the hardest. O Destiny,
on me and on my house now heavily you trod,
a sudden plague-spot sent by some avenging god,
a grinding weight of calamities!
A sea of troubles, alas, I see
so wide I never shall swim clear of it again
nor rise above the climbing billows of this pain.
What can I find to say? Where are the words to name
this heavy fate of yours, my wife, my love?
Vanishing out of my hand like a bird in flight,
leaping so rapidly down into Hades' night!
Terrible stroke of Fortune! And what is to blame,
if not some far-off long-forgot ancestral crime
that, guided by the powers above,
has overtaken me in later time?

FIRST MEMBER OF CHORUS

My lord, such grief comes not to you alone,
and many other men have lost good wives.

THESEUS

> I would be underground now. I want to die,
> and dwell in darkness there underground,
> now I no longer have your dearest company.
> You did not merely die; you murdered you and me.
> Will no one speak? no one tell me why
> that death-bound, pitiful impulse found
> its way into your heart, my dear? Will no one say
> why it was done? For nothing, then, these halls display
> throngs of my faithful slaves? Oh I am nothing now,
> because of you! This agony of sight
> my life cannot endure, my tongue cannot express.
> My house is empty now, my children motherless.
> Gone from us, gone, my dearest! Ah, why did you go
> from us, O best of women whom the shining sun
> or flashing of the stars of night
> has looked or ever shall look down upon!

CHORUS

> 2. O poor man, poor man, for your stricken home!
> 1. Oh my eyes for your sorrow are wet
> with tears and yet
> I dread a grief that still may come!

THESEUS

> Look, look!
> Whatever can this tablet be tied here
> to her dear hand? Perhaps it wants to give
> some sign, some reason? But perhaps she wrote
> a letter pleading for her marriage-bed
> and for her sons. Poor Phaedra, have no fear:
> there lives no woman who will share the bed
> and house of Theseus now. See how the signs,
> pressed from her signet-ring of hammered gold
> by this same hand of her who is no more,
> coax me to read. Then let me, once I have

unwound the strings that bind it from their seals,
see what this tablet wants to say to me.

★

CHORUS

1. Alas! again the gods pause not but give
   woe after woe!
2. I could not live
   a life so harried by destiny's sway!
3. Alas! I say that the house of my king
   no longer is, it is passed away!
5. O gods, if it may be, still spare this house!
   (*indicating* THESEUS)
4. Over there I see, as a prophet knows
   an evil bird, more evil threatening!

★

THESEUS

Oh what disaster on disaster comes!—
not to be borne or spoken! This to me!

CHORUS

What is the matter? Tell me, if you will.

THESEUS (*chanted*)

The tablet shouts, shouts for revenge! Oh where
shall I turn from the weight of this wrong?
I am driven down to my death!
I have learned what a song! what a song!
from this letter as if it had breath!

CHORUS

So much, let out, heralds a host of woes.

THESEUS (*chanted*)

I shall hold it no longer inside the gates
of speech, a wrong that overwhelms and devastates—
my people, hear!
(*spoken*)

Hippolytus has dared to touch my bed
with force, despising the dread eye of Zeus.
But O my father! O Poseidon! You
who promised me three curses once, of these
use one to kill my son, let him not live
beyond this day, if those curses be real
and valid which you long since granted me!

FIRST MEMBER OF CHORUS

My lord! I beg, call back that curse again!
You'll soon find you are wrong. Trust me for this!

THESEUS

I'll not recall it. More: I banish him
out of this land, so that of two fates one
at least will strike him. Either Poseidon will
honor my curses, kill him, send him down
into the gates of Hades, or, cast out
from Troezen, and a vagabond, he shall
in strange lands drain a thin life to the dregs!

FIRST MEMBER OF CHORUS

Here is your son himself, and in good time:
Hippolytus. Relax your stubborn rage,
my lord. Think what will do your house most good.
 (*Enter* HIPPOLYTUS)

HIPPOLYTUS

Father, I came in haste, hearing your cries.
Over what sorrow you at present groan
I do not know, but I should like to hear
the cause from you. But what is this I see?
Your wife—my father—dead! But this is most
bewildering! She whom I left just now,
who looked upon this light no long time past!
Whatever happened! How did she meet death?
Father, I want to hear the story from you.
But you say nothing? Silence is no help

in trouble. For a heart hungry as mine
to hear all that concerns you will be found
to have a greedy palate for your woes.
You should not keep your problems from your friends,
Father, and more than friends. It is not right.

THESEUS

Mankind! Your utmost efforts are in vain!
Why do you teach ten thousand kinds of skill,
invent all things, discover everything,
when you have never learned nor hunted out
a way to teach the mindless how to think?

HIPPOLYTUS

What a stupendous sophist he would be
indeed, who forced the thoughtless kind to think!
But, Father, is your small talk not ill-timed?
I fear your sorrows drive your tongue too far.

THESEUS

Ah, mortal men should have some certain sign
by which to tell their friends and know their minds,
which one is a true friend and which is not.
All men should have two voices quite distinct—
an honest one, the other—as might be—
so we might test the one intending wrong
against the just one, and not be deceived.

HIPPOLYTUS

But—has some friend of yours breathed in your ear
something against me, thus infecting me
when I have done no harm? Father, I am
amazed at you. Your words astonish me,
so shifting and unsettled in your mind.

THESEUS

Alas, the human mind! Where will it lead?
Where will there come a limit to insolence,
to shameless daring? If it still goes on

swelling from one man's lifetime to the next,
each later generation being far
more excellent in evil than the last,
the gods will have to, add another earth
to this one, so there will be room to hold
the misbegotten and the villainous!
Look at this man: my son, whom I begot,
who has defiled my bed, and who is proved
plainly by this dead woman to be vile!
Don't turn away! Since you have come this far
into contagion, turn your face this way,
here, toward your father! And this is you,
this most superior man who walks with gods?
You, you the virtuous one, unstained by sin?
Far be it from me to credit your fine claims,
for I should be imputing to the gods
a desperate ignorance and want of sense!
Now put on airs! Go peddle your pure food
of vegetables lacking little souls!
Take Orpheus for your master, revel in
rare ecstasies and treasure up the fumes
of many scriptures! You now stand exposed.
I here declare to all: avoid such men,
for they are up to no good with their grave
and priestly verbiage, scheming infamy!
      (*brandishing the tablet*)
Look, she is dead. Do you imagine this
will save you? No, for this convicts you most,
vilest of men! What oaths, what arguments
can be more powerful than she is now
and clear you of this charge? Ah, you will **say**
she hated you because bastards are born
at war with the legitimate. But then
you make her a poor bargainer in life,

to sacrifice the dearest thing she had
to your hostility. Or would you say
erotic folly is not born in men,
but is in women? I have known young men
no less susceptible than women are
when Aphrodite shakes their growing minds,
and being male they can accomplish more.
But why contend with arguments of yours
when witness of the plainest kind is borne
by this dead body? Get out of this land!
At once, to banishment! Never come near
my city of Athens founded by the gods
nor any borders that my spear commands!
If I accept defeat, wronged thus by you,
the brigand Siris never will admit
I killed him, but will call my boast a lie;
the rocks fronting the sea where Sciron died
will say the wicked never felt my weight.

FIRST MEMBER OF CHORUS

How shall I say that any mortal man
succeeds, when here the foremost are hurled back?

HIPPOLYTUS

Father, your anger and your mind made up
so stubbornly are terrible to face.
Yet, though your case does have good arguments,
if one unfold it all, it is not good.
I do not flatter myself that I can speak
before a crowd, being far more adept
at speaking to my friends, of my own age,
and to but few of them. And this is fair,
since those who count for nothing with the wise
are more inspired to speak before a mob.
Yet I am forced, since this emergency
has come upon me, to loosen my tongue.

And first of all I shall begin to speak
to that point where you first attacked, as if
to end me, finding me with no defense.
You see that sun? this earth? They have not seen
any man born more virtuous than I,
deny it as you will. For first, I know
how to revere the gods, and choose my friends
among such men as try to do no wrong
but who would be ashamed not to inform
on evil and requite ignoble deeds
with treachery—I do not mock my friends,
but am as frank when with them as away,
yet quite immune from one thing, this same charge
you think you now convict me of, for I
up to this day have kept my body pure.
I know that act only from what I hear
or see in pictures—and I'm not too fond
of seeing them, having a virgin soul.
My virtue still has not persuaded you?
Still you must prove what has corrupted me.
Perhaps her body was more beautiful
than any other woman's? Or perhaps
I hoped I might possess your royal house,
once I acquired its heiress and her bed?
If so, I was impractical, or mad.
Or say that it is sweet to be a king—
not for the wise, though it may turn the head
of any mortal who likes primacy.
I'd like, in winning the Olympic games,
to be the first, but second in the state,
and always be successful, having friends
of the best people. Thus one may have wealth,
and, not being feared, more popularity
than if one had the sovereignty itself.

One thing I have not said; the rest you've heard:
if I had here a witness true as I,
and *she* were living, as I plead my case,
then you would find the guilty through the facts,
but as it is, I take my oath by Zeus,
patron of oaths, and by the earth we tread,
that never have I touched your marriage-bed,
nor wanted to, nor ever thought of it.
So may I perish without name or fame,
homeless and countryless and wandering
in exile on the earth, and may the sea
and land alike refuse to take this flesh
when I am dead, if I was born so base.
But if this woman died for fear of me—
I do not know. And I am bound by right
to speak no further. She controlled herself,
who had no self-control, and I, who can
control myself, have done so, to my harm.

FIRST MEMBER OF CHORUS (*alarmed*)
You have already said enough to turn
away the charge, and taken by the gods
your oath, which is of no small cogency!

THESEUS
Is this man not a born singer of spells,
a vocal wizard, who thinks he can rule
my heart with his bland equanimity,
after dishonoring his father so!

HIPPOLYTUS
I am astonished at that very thing,
Father, in you; for if you were my son
and I your father, I would have killed you,
not merely made you pay with banishment
if you had ever dared to touch my wife.

THESEUS

> How right you are! But you shall not die thus,
> as you have laid the law down for yourself—
> a quick death is the easiest one for him
> who merely is unfortunate, but you
> shall, wandering outcast from your fatherland,
> in strange lands drain a thin life to the dregs:
> such are the wages of the impious man!

HIPPOLYTUS

> What will you do? Will you not wait for Time
> to inform against me, but exile me now?

THESEUS

> Beyond the seas which end the East and West,
> if I were able, I so loathe your looks!

HIPPOLYTUS

> Will you discount all pledges, oaths, and signs
> read by the priests, and banish me untried?

THESEUS

> This tablet, though no prophet has subscribed
> an omen to it, still accuses you
> with perfect certainty. And to your birds
> wandering overhead I say fare you well!

HIPPOLYTUS

> You gods! why may I not speak out at last,
> being destroyed by you I reverence?
> No no! For I should not persuade at all
> those I have need to, and to no avail
> I should make nothing of the vows I swore.

THESEUS

> You kill me with your sanctimoniousness!
> Go now, right now, out of your father's land!

HIPPOLYTUS

> But where then shall I turn? What foreign friend
> will take me in, exiled on such a charge?

THESEUS

> Why, everyone who welcomes to his home
> seducers and defilers of men's wives,
> those who will keep him company in crime.

HIPPOLYTUS

> Ah, this comes near the heart and near to tears—
> to pass for vile—and you believe I am!

THESEUS

> You should have groaned and wept and looked ahead
> then, when you dared abuse your father's wife!

HIPPOLYTUS

> O house, if you could utter forth a voice
> in witness whether I'm a wicked man!

THESEUS (*pointing to body of* PHAEDRA)

> Splendid! We'll take to voiceless witnesses:
> this fact says nothing, yet it proves you vile.

HIPPOLYTUS

> Alas!
> If *I* could only stand there opposite
> and look upon myself, so I might weep
> to see what great injustice I endure!

THESEUS

> Indeed your discipline has rather been
> rapt worship of yourself, than to fulfill
> the pieties due your parents, and be just.

HIPPOLYTUS

> Oh, my poor mother! Oh, that bitter birth!
> May none I care for have a bastard's life!

THESEUS

> Drag him away, you slaves! Did you not hear
> when I pronounced him alien to this land?

HIPPOLYTUS

> Let any of them who touches me beware!
> Yourself, if you desire to, thrust me out!

THESEUS

> I *will* do that, if you do not obey
> my words alone. For no pity at all
> comes stealing over me for your exile!
>> *(Exit into the palace)*

HIPPOLYTUS

> So then, it is decided. Oh, how hard,
> knowing the truth of this, not to know how
> to tell it. Dearest of the gods to me,
> daughter of Leto, thou my confidante,
> my close companion in the hunt, today
> I flee from Athens' glorious realm. Farewell,
> O people of Erechtheus and his land!
> O plain of Troezen, how much happiness
> you hold for those who grow to manhood here!
> Farewell! I speak to you and see you now
> for the last time. Come with me, you young men
> who grew up with me here, escort me now
> out of the country, bidding me farewell.
> For you will never see another man
> more virtuous and more self-controlled than I,
> although my father thinks it is not so.

(Exit, followed by a few companions. Others remain to sing the first strophes of the chorus, during which they too gradually go out.)

★

CHORUS

(Male)　　　　　　　　　　　　　　　　　　　　　　　*(a)*

> Ah, when it enters my mind that the gods have a care
>> for us, then
> what respite from pain!
> Yet I hope for a meaning in vain,

left here to stare at the drifting fortunes and actions of
    men.
Everything changes around without rest
and the wandering life of mankind at the best
must move again and again.

(Female)   *(a′)*

Oh if my luck and the gods were to answer my prayer
        and my need
for wealth and success,
for a spirit unstained by distress,
keeping a not overstrict and still not a counterfeit creed!
Had I a character easy to change
day to day to meet anything sudden or strange
my life were one I might bless!

★

(Male)   *(b)*

Now a new sight so appalls me my spirit no longer runs
        clear,
now I have seen the brightest star
ever risen on Athens or Hellas driven afar
through his father's anger afar into other lands!
Oh have we not seen him disappear,
O you shores near the city!
1, 2, 5. O glittering sands,
O you hills where the groves and the oaktrees are,
where he finished the kill in the midst of his hounds and
        his men
and holy Artemis was with him then.
        (*Exit* MALE CHORUS)

(Female)   *(b′)*

1. Never again will he mount on his chariot, reining his
        fast

Venetian colts to hold the course
around Limna with pounding of expert pacing of horse.

2. In the palace the music that sang in his fine-strung lyre,
never asleep, is asleep at last.

3. And the green glades where Artemis loved to retire
will no longer be graced with his crowns of flowers.

4. And without you the battles of girls to be chosen the one
to share your bed and be your bride are done.
   (with nubility)

5. And I shall lead weeping a life not to be led!   *(Epode)*
Mother, poor Mother, what was the good
of giving me birth, alas! if I live unwed?
I would rave at the gods if I could!
Oh oh! You three Graces who bind couples in one,
why have you sent the poor prince from his hall,
from his fatherland, when he has done
nothing to harm us at all?

★

FIRST MEMBER OF CHORUS
     Wait, look! A servant of Hippolytus
     comes rushing this way with a scowling face!
          (Enter MESSENGER*)*

MESSENGER
     Women, where should I go to find the king
     of this land, Theseus? Show me, if you know.
     Or is he just inside the palace here?
          *(*THESEUS, *in black, comes out)*

FIRST MEMBER OF CHORUS
     There he is now, just coming through the doors.

MESSENGER
     Theseus, I bring a story that deserves

extreme concern, to you and to all those
who are Athenian citizens or dwell
within the limits of Troezenian soil.

THESEUS

What is it? Has still more disaster seized
on both of our two neighboring city-states?

MESSENGER

Hippolytus is dead. One may say so,
though in some little measure he still lives.

THESEUS

Who killed him? I suppose it was someone
who sought him out in hatred and whose wife
he had abused, like mine, by violence.

MESSENGER

Four chariot-horses he had trained himself,
at home, have killed him, and the curse you sent
out of your mouth, and prayed the god of seas,
your father, to bring down upon your son.

THESEUS

O Gods! Poseidon! thou has been a true
father to me, to hearken to my curse!
Tell me, how did he die? How did the club
of Justice crush him who dishonored me?

MESSENGER

Some of us, near the breakers of the beach,
were currying the horses' manes with combs
and weeping, since the word had come to us
that no more might Hippolytus set foot
in Troezen, being exiled and destitute
by your decree. And then he came himself
with the same tearful song to sing to us
upon the shore. A numberless gathering
of friends of his own age attended him.
At length he stopped lamenting and he said,

"Why complain aimlessly? I must obey.
Yoke up the horses to my chariot,
my slaves. This city is now dead to me."
Then every man of us went right to work
and quicker than it takes to tell of it
we had the mares in harness and led up
beside the master. Then he caught the reins
up from the rail and set his feet astride,
still in their hunting-boots. But first he stretched
his arms out to the gods and said, "O Zeus,
if I was born so evil, let me die!
And let my father realize at last
how he has wronged me, whether I am dead
or still alive to look upon the sun!"
With that he took the barbed whip in his hand
and touched the mares all with a single stroke,
and we attendants ran beside the team,
close by the bits, accompanying him
straight down the road which leads to Argos and
to Epidaurus. We drove out upon
an uninhabited stretch, where there's a shore
touching your borders and yet facing out
on the Saronic gulf. There came a roar
from underground like thunder sent by Zeus,
a heavy rumbling it chilled our blood to hear.
Straight up the horses reared their heads, their ears,
toward heaven. A strong young terror took hold of us,
where ever that sound might come from. When we looked
off toward the foaming shores we saw a wave
prodigious, holy, lifted up to heaven,
so the Scironian headlands disappeared
before my eyes. The Isthmus and the rock
named for Asclepius were hid. The wave
swelled then still higher and, spouting roundabout

great bursts of foam and whistling blasts of spray,
rushed for the shore, straight at the chariot
and its four horses. Then the triple crest
crashed into breakers, and cast forth a bull,
a wild portentous thing, whose bellowing filled
the coast, which bellowed back a shuddering sound.
To us who looked upon him, the bull seemed
a sight beyond the strength of human eyes.
At once a panic fell upon the team;
their master, well accustomed to the ways
of horses, seized the reins in both his hands
and pulled, as men on shipboard pull an oar,
hanging his whole weight backward on the reins.
The mares set their jaws hard on the forged bits
and carried him by force, not turning back
for all his oarsman's hand, nor for the reins,
nor for the chariot when it dragged or caught.
And if, still holding to the helm, he steered
their course toward even ground, the bull appeared
in front, to turn them back, setting the team
out of their minds with fear. If they plunged on
into the rocks with frenzied hearts, then he
quietly followed them, beside the rail,
until he made them suddenly rear and fling
their manes up and upset the chariot
when they had driven its wheels hard against
a rock. Then all was tangled and confused.
Up in the air flew bolts and spokes of the wheels
and axle-pins. And poor Hippolytus,
wound in the reins, was dragged along, being tied
by bonds that would not loosen, in the dust,
dashing his head against the rocks, tearing
his flesh, and howling dreadful cries to hear—
"Stop! Stop! You mares fed at my cribs! Do not

CHORUS

And here the poor man drags along at length
the wreck of his youthful flesh and his strength
and the sullied gold of his head, alas;
alas for the double grief that has
been destined to come to the royal hall!
The gods have at last fulfilled it all.

(*Enter* HIPPOLYTUS, *helped along by his companions*)

HIPPOLYTUS

Ay ay!
Ay me! to be dragged, ground in the dust
by a curse unjust, by a sire unjust!
I am lost, crushed! Ay me!
Through my head runs pain upon pain!
Ah the death-pangs leap through my brain!
Stop! I shall rest. My body will not stand.

(*Lets himself down*)

Ah. Ah.
O vicious team of horses fed
by my own hand,
you mangled me and left for dead.

(*The slaves try to help him rise*)

Ah no! Ah no!
Slaves, steadily, firmly, when you take
hold of this raw flesh, gently, for the gods' sake!

(*angrily*)

Who came there, touching my right side?
Raise me up easily, carefully, pull all together,
raise me, outcast and accursed, who have died
for the sins of my father!
Zeus! Zeus! Do *you* see this?
This, this is I, devout and reverent,
this, this is I, above all others virtuous,
who now move into death, which is

before my eyes, under the earth, leaving my life, thus.
And all in vain I spent
with hand and mind
my labors and my pieties
before mankind.
Ay ay! Again
the pain, the pain!
Let go! Ah let me go!
Why is this Healer, Death, so slow?
Help kill me! Ah! Kill me, and here
end the doom that hunts me down! I long
for some two-edged and whetted spear
to run me through
and lay this life of mine asleep!
Ah my father's merciless curses keep
the course of evil due
from an ancient wrong
done by blood-stained men of my blood
and my forebears long ago;
it has not delayed, it is not withstood,
it has reached me now!
Why? when I never did anything wrong?
Ay me! What shall I say?
How shall I get my life away
from this relentless suffering?
Oh come, you black necessity
of death, on your nocturnal wing,
send me to sleep, come comfort me!

★

ARTEMIS

Poor friend! With what misfortunes you are yoked!
Nobility of mind has ruined you.

HIPPOLYTUS

Oh, there!
O breath of heavenly fragrance! Even now,
even in my pain I feel thee, and my body
is once again made light. Oh, is she here,
the goddess Artemis, here, in this place?

ARTEMIS

Poor friend! With what misfortunes you are yoked!

HIPPOLYTUS

You see me, lady, how it is with me?

ARTEMIS

I see. But tears may not fall from my eyes.

HIPPOLYTUS

You have no servant now to lead your dogs . . .

ARTEMIS

No, none. But very dear to me you die.

HIPPOLYTUS

to tend your steeds, to guard your images . . .

ARTEMIS

Unscrupulous Aphrodite worked this out.

HIPPOLYTUS

Alas! I know the power which ruined me now!

ARTEMIS

You slighted her. Your virtue angered her.

HIPPOLYTUS

I see. Love has destroyed all three of us.

ARTEMIS

Your father, you, and third, your father's wife.

HIPPOLYTUS

Oh I have groaned even for my father's plight.

ARTEMIS

He was deceived by a designing god.

HIPPOLYTUS

O Father, how I pity you for this!

THESEUS

        I'm done, my child. Life holds no charm for me.

HIPPOLYTUS

        Your error brings more sorrow on you than me.

THESEUS

        If I could die, my child, instead of you!

HIPPOLYTUS

        What bitter gifts your father's were to you!

THESEUS

        If they had never come into my mouth!

HIPPOLYTUS

        What then? You'd still have killed me, in your wrath.

THESEUS

        Yes, for the gods had driven my mind astray.

HIPPOLYTUS

        Alas!

        If mankind's curses could but reach the gods!

ARTEMIS

        Leave off! For even in the gloom below
        the wrath of Aphrodite which she hurled
        fiercely against your body for the sake
        of your too-reverent and virtuous mind,
        shall not go unrequited, for my hand
        shall pay this back upon some other man
        who is to her the dearest of mankind,
        with this bow which has never missed its mark.
        And to repay you for these sufferings
        the greatest honors Troezen has to give
        I give to you. For its unmarried girls
        shall give you, till they marry, locks of their hair,
        and through long ages you shall harvest in
        their greatest grief, their many tears. Always
        lamenting songs of virgins will be sung
        about you, nor shall Phaedra's love for you

pass into silence and oblivion.
But you, O son of ancient Aegeus, take
your child into your arms, and hold him close.
You did not mean to kill him. Men may well
do wrong when gods determine what they do.
And you, Hippolytus, I bid you not
to hate your father. You now know the fate
by which you perish. And with this farewell,
because I may not look upon the dead
nor stain my eyes with the last gasps of death,
and I see you already close to it.

HIPPOLYTUS

Farewell, you too, departing, affluent maid!
Quitting with ease our long companionship!
My quarrel with my father, since you ask,
I willingly forego, as in the past
I have obeyed your every word. Ay ay!
The dark already comes over my eyes.
Father, hold me, and lift my body up.

THESEUS

Alas, my child, what are you doing to me!

HIPPOLYTUS

I die. Already I see the gates of death.

THESEUS

Ah, will you leave my hand so stained with guilt?

HIPPOLYTUS

No, Father. I absolve you of my death.

THESEUS

What do you say? You set me free of blood?

HIPPOLYTUS

Yes, by the virgin goddess of the bow.

THESEUS

My dearest son! Ah what a true-born son
you prove yourself unto your father now!

HIPPOLYTUS
>   Pray to have lawful sons as true as I.

THESEUS
>   Alas! Alas! Your good, your reverent, mind!

HIPPOLYTUS
>   Farewell you too, my father, fare you well.

THESEUS
>   Do not forsake me now, my child! Be strong!

HIPPOLYTUS
>   My strength is overpowered. Father, I die.
>   Cover my face up quickly now with robes.

THESEUS
>   Oh splendid lands of Athens, of the god
>   Pallas Athena, what a man you lose!
>   And I, alas! O Aphrodite, I
>   forever after shall recall your crimes!

(*He has covered the body with the black cloak. For the proscenium stage there can be a pietà effect downstage. Otherwise the body is carried into the palace by* THESEUS *and* SLAVES *during the final chorus.*)

★

CHORUS
>   On all our citizens this common woe
>   came without warning.
>   Many a plashing tear must flow.
>   Word of the great brought low
>   brings greater cause of mourning.

EXEUNT

TRANSLATOR'S NOTE

The stage directions, since they do not exist in the Greek text, have been supplied by the translator. The translation was done primarily for production with music by George Lynn, so the stage directions often go rather beyond inference from the text.

The only egregious departure from the usual staging is in having Artemis appear not bodily but as a voice in the air. There is no direct evidence about this in the Greek, one way or another. But at the beginning of the play Hippolytus says that he is privileged to hear the voice of the goddess though not to see her. At the end, when dying, he evidently hears her and even smells her, but makes no comment on having a vision of her at last. Such a vision would, I believe, require some exclamation, so I infer she does not appear. The projection of divine voices over something like our public-address system was quite possible in the Greek theatre, but that is too long a story for discussion here. Anyone is welcome to prefer a visible goddess in the regular machine or on foot. And see page 75.

The translation is indebted mainly to Paley's edition, to the Loeb edition, and to the Oxford text.

THE HIPPOLYTUS OF DRAMA AND MYTH

by

HAZEL E. BARNES

THE DRAMA

When Aristotle stated that Euripides was the most tragic of the tragedians, he apparently was referring merely to the high proportion of unhappy endings found in Euripides' plays. But there is a more profound sense in which the statement is true. Euripides is the most tragic of the Greek dramatists for the same reason that we find him to be the most modern; that is, because his characters move in a world of shifting values where even the central issues are not clear. With Sophocles too, of course, the conflict may be between two "rights" rather than between a good and an evil. Both Antigone and Philoctetes are caught between loyalty to the state and duty to the demands of conscience in an individual instance where the state is wrong. Similarly Aeschylus' Orestes is torn between piety toward one parent and pity for another. Still even in these examples the issue is, as it were, externalized. The characters' decisions are made deliberately as the result of an intellectual appraisal of conflicting claims. There is no question of willing one thing and doing another; tragedy is not the result of irrational forces within the psyche. It was Euripides who first portrayed the full drama of the mystery of the human person.

Hippolytus is in many ways a paradox. Its plot, a mingling of the fatal triangle and Potiphar's wife themes, has been treated by the dramatist in such a way as to highlight its universality, becoming indeed a study of fundamental forces so completely delineated as hardly to need more than allegorical types to em-

71

body the basic struggle. Yet there is no play of Euripides in which the characters are more sharply individualized. The story is so humanly probable that divine intervention is gratuitous; yet two deities dominate the action from beginning to end. Moreover, Euripides has combined with this universal plot and this mythological apparatus some of his sharpest and most specific satire directed against both the conventional mythology and the rationalistic arguments of contemporary philosophy.

One thing at least seems clear. Euripides must have been interested both in the individual characters of his drama, the *personally* human, and in the symbolic, universal aspects of the underlying conflict. Hence it would be a mistake either to regard the divine figures as so much impedimenta or to expect any of the characters to function only as a one-meaning symbol or type. Just as with Dante's *Divine Comedy,* we will have to read the play on more than one level, but the layers cannot always be kept distinct. We may on occasion find Euripides actually adopting one plane as a point of view from which to criticize his creations on another.

The most literal reading of the play would take the mythological framework at face value. Very probably one purpose among others of Euripides is that we should so read the story and see just what the conventional mythology may reveal concerning the nature of two of its most important figures. Obviously on this level Euripides is pure satirist. He criticizes the Olympians on moral grounds as unworthy the worship of decent human beings. That he is serious in this attack many comparable passages in other plays will bear witness, and we can, I think, detect in him a certain relish as he drives his point home.

Of course the unadorned plot itself is sufficiently damning. Out of pique and hurt pride Aphrodite, jealous because Hippolytus refuses to worship her and spends all his time adoring Artemis, resolves to punish him. Thus she causes Phaedra, his young stepmother, to fall in love with him, for Aphrodite is suf-

ficiently a psychologist and a prophet to foresee that this passion
will destroy both mortals. In answer to the inevitable question
as to why the innocent Phaedra should have to suffer, Aphrodite
says,

> And Phaedra, though her honor
> is yet unblemished,[1] still must also die.
> For her misfortune shall not count with me
> more than exacting from my enemies
> punishment on the scale I owe myself.

Granted that such unrelieved self-interest is woven into the original myth, it is notable that Euripides points up the fact rather
than seeking any palliative excuse. Certainly Aphrodite might
as a powerful goddess have found some other way of ruining
Hippolytus without destroying the guiltless. But she does not
try, nor does Euripides make any attempt to justify the goddess'
choice of Phaedra as her instrument. More of typically Euripidean satire occurs when the Nurse, after her first shocked reaction to Phaedra's tale of love, tries to persuade her mistress
that after all, illicit love is at least no unheard-of crime. The
gods too, she argues, have had their famous amours—and with
mortals too. She names Semele and Cephalus as examples.

> Yet *they* stay on in heaven
> and never try to break free from their gods,
> having grown fond of being overcome,
> I daresay, by misfortune of this kind.
> But you will not endure it? Then your sire
> should have begotten you on other terms

---

[1] The Greek here is ἢ δ' εὐκλεὴς μέν, ἀλλ' ὅμως ἀπόλλυται. The line is sometimes
taken as referring to the future, stating that Phaedra will die honorably, though
die she must. This interpretation seems to me wrong, both because it is a less
accurate translation of the Greek and because it is untrue. Phaedra does not die
honorably. She has been scorned by Hippolytus, and her illicit passion is about
to be made common knowledge.

> and under other gods than those we have,
> if you will not accept these easy ways.

The Nurse goes on to say that Phaedra's will to be chaste is a blameworthy desire to surpass the gods themselves.

> Leave off your wicked thoughts, leave off your pride,
> since it is nothing but excessive pride,
> this wish to be superior to the gods.
> Be brave—as a god wills it—brave in love.

Even allowing for the sophistry in the Nurse's speech (which Phaedra is quick to detect), we must note that the description of heavenly morality is allowed to stand. Phaedra obviously regards this sort of thing as no fit model for her own conduct, but she accepts the picture.

It might be argued that Aphrodite's action was justified at least partially by Hippolytus' overt scorn. But even here we must not forget the words of the old servant to her:

> For the gods
> must have more wisdom than we mortals have.

Similarly Poseidon's granting of Theseus' wish for Hippolytus' destruction might be excused on the basis of his having sworn to grant *any* three wishes of Theseus and his feeling that the King deserved to suffer for his rash impulse (though this would not justify sacrificing Hippolytus). The portrait of Artemis, however, leaves no doubt that Euripides' intent was to cast aspersions on the Olympians. By right Artemis should be one of the heroines of the play. In part she too is one of Aphrodite's victims. She has lost the worshiper she cherished, and she must endure the shame of having been proved helpless to aid him. There was a chance here, if he had wanted it, for Euripides to have presented a great sympathetic portrait of the goddess as a divinity capable of love for humanity and able to suffer, bringing comfort to the afflicted, depicting the joys promised the faithful as a counterbalance to the misery inflicted by Aphrodite on the unbelieving. Since some versions of the myth allowed it, Artemis might even have turned Hippolytus' death into religious triumph by a promise of resurrection. Evidently Euripides did not want it this way, and what do we have? One of the nastiest creatures ever to have claimed Olympian provenance!

Upon her first appearance to Theseus Artemis launches into violent reproaches, obviously enjoying the torture she is inflicting.[2]

> Hear, Theseus, the full roster of your woes—
> I'll spare you none of them. I mean to hurt.

Unsympathetically and with emphasis on Theseus' easy gullibility, she reveals the true account of Phaedra's love and death, gives Theseus time only for a despairing groan, and goes gleefully on.

> That story bites you to the quick? Be still
> and hear the rest, so you will groan the more.

Hereupon Artemis informs the already frenzied Theseus that along with knowing himself to be responsible for his son's

---

[2]Although Hippolytus, in the name of his Artemis-ideal, is fanatical enough in his rejection of the physical side of life, I cannot agree with Donald Sutherland that Euripides went so far as to deny the goddess herself a body. To me the visible presence of Aphrodite at the beginning of the play demands the appearance of her opposite at the end—dramatically and in the interests of aesthetic balance. Presumably she is on the roof of the palace, alighting from her trip through the sky via the traditional stage machine. Her distance from the dying Hippolytus and his own weakness would sufficiently explain his not seeing her. He gives no sign of noticing Theseus either until after Artemis' speech. Professor Sutherland feels that the goddess' aloof divinity is best represented by her total lack of incarnation. I believe that her finicky reluctance to look on the dying and her readiness to abide strictly by Olympian regulations are more effective if she is poised daintily on the housetop, impatient to be off before death and mourning take over. (See p. 67.)

death, he must realize that his misuse of Poseidon's gift has won
his own father's hatred. At last when Theseus wants only to
die, Artemis slightly relents.

> Your deeds are terrible,
> yet you can be forgiven even them,
> for Aphrodite willed these things to be,
> to glut her anger.

To satiate her still greater resentment toward Aphrodite, Artemis
will admit that Theseus was not wholly to blame. The goddess
has another reason as well: she must justify herself for not
intervening to clear up matters until after it was too late. Her
excuse is that the gods are not allowed to interfere with each
other's fixed purpose. Fear of Zeus kept her from attempting
any action. (Artemis is no Prometheus!)

> So that you may be sure
> that had I not stood in terror of Zeus
> I never should have let myself be shamed
> so dreadfully as this, to let him die
> who was my dearest friend of all mankind.

Even here Artemis seems to be concerned about her reputation
as the champion of her devotee more than she is for her worshiper himself. Her one expression of sorrow is so general as
to sound almost impersonal and is accompanied by a statement
so flagrantly in contradiction with the existing situation that
I cannot believe Euripides was unaware of its ironic inappro-
priateness.

> I also grieve. The gods
> do not rejoice to see the righteous die.
> It is the wicked whom we extirpate
> completely, with their homes and children too.

The final scene adds perfecting touches to this disagreeable portrait. Artemis tells Hippolytus that he is dear to her but that she is not allowed to weep for him. She herself condemns the unscrupulous Aphrodite but is quick to check Hippolytus' despairing wish:

> If mankind's curses could but reach the gods!

Then Artemis offers compensation—certain ritualistic honors after death and the promise that she personally will see to it that one of Aphrodite's favorites (Adonis?) comes to an untimely death. Apparently it is the gods' destructive purposes which cannot be blocked, not the benevolent! Finally Artemis departs with the explanation that she is not permitted to pollute her eyes with the sight of death. One sentence in the goddess' last speech sounds inconsistent with her sadistic denunciation of Theseus earlier. At the point where she bids Hippolytus forgive his father, Artemis says,

> Men may well
> do wrong when gods determine what they do.

This implied criticism of the Olympians, which is almost an echo of the Nurse's arguments, does not suit the goddess. It sounds rather like Euripides' own comment on the situation, a final moral judgment. Such an evaluation seems to be borne out further by two things. First, there is never any repentance on the part of Hippolytus so far as Aphrodite is concerned, no acknowledgement that his punishment is deserved. Even Theseus' last line,

> O Aphrodite, I
> forever after shall recall your crimes!

is as much a denunciation as a recognition of Aphrodite's power. Second and still more significant is Hippolytus' disillusioned comment upon Artemis' withdrawal:

> Farewell, you too, departing, affluent maid!
> Quitting with ease our long companionship.

On the purely mythological level the play may be read as consistent with Euripides' general attitude toward the Olympians. While I do not believe that a satire on popular anthropomorphic concepts of the gods is the primary purpose of the drama, I think that it is there intentionally as one layer of meaning. Actually it is a fairly weighty attack.

Obviously we cannot limit ourselves to such a literal approach; to do so would make mere puppets out of the characters and render meaningless their rich personalities. The alternative is not merely to dismiss the divine opponents as satiric caricatures and to concentrate exclusively on the human individuals. For it seems certain that beneath the anthropomorphic masks the deities represent fundamental conflicting forces which Euripides held to be of vital importance, whether they exist within the human psyche or externalized in the universal nature of things. As the Nurse says to Phaedra,

> This Aphrodite is no god at all,
> but surely something greater than a god,
> who has destroyed her and me and this house.

Aphrodite, of course, stands for the principle of sex. In a very broad sense she might be said also to parallel the figure of Dionysus in the *Bacchae,* thus becoming almost a symbol of a primitive life force. Artemis is a little more difficult to place. Are we to think of her purely negatively as the refusal to recognize the irrational in man? In that case she is hardly necessary; Hippolytus himself might have served as the foil to Aphrodite as Pentheus did to Dionysus. If we seek in her a more positive image, she symbolizes perhaps the ascetic ideal, purity, mental and spiritual self-discipline. Another way of putting it would be to say that Aphrodite represents that impulse in man which causes him to find self-fulfillment in emotional and physical contact with others, Artemis the yearning for self-sufficiency, the desire to keep one's inward being isolate from an encroachment by others which is felt to be a violation.

On what we might thus call the allegorical or even metaphysical level, the principal characters are hardly three-dimensional human beings. But whereas they were mere puppets to the deities anthropomorphically conceived, they have now become rather types, personal embodiments of the forces for which the goddesses are symbols. Here a curious thing has happened. Among the many functions performed by the gods for the early Greeks, at least one was that of serving as an object onto which humans might "project" their own emotional motivations.[3] When Helen's infatuation had led her to run off with Paris, Priam told her not to blame herself, for it was entirely Aphrodite who was responsible. When Achilles' own better judgment cautioned him not to yield to his impulse to strike Agamemnon, Homer tells us that Athena dragged him back by the hair and forbade his rash act. But nobody except Achilles saw her. Similar examples are numerous. It is little wonder that the Greeks attributed to external gods both the overpowering impulses which seemed at times to force them to behave in ways which later reflection pronounced foreign to their basic attitudes, and, on the other hand, the inward voice which seemed to come from a distance and dictate counsel which was unwelcome. The present tendency to make subconscious motivations wholly autonomous and in a sense external to the conscious ego is not after all so very different. In the case of Euripides we might, of course, see simply another manifestation of this same projection. But for him in fifth-century Athens such projection would be self-conscious and deliberate. Personally I think that he is doing precisely the reverse, that he is beginning with the abstract

---

[3]For a full discussion of this view, see E. R. Dodds, *The Greeks and the Irrational* (Berkeley: University of California Press, 1951), especially Chapter One, "Agamemnon's Apology."

concept, then watching to see what happens when humans domi-
nated by opposing principles meet with each other.

Naturally any reconciliation between goddesses symbolizing
such diametrically opposed ideals is impossible, and Euripides
represents their enmity as destined to continue after the play is
ended. Though we should probably be right in assuming that
he would agree that some balance between the two is necessary
for man's well-being, I do not think that Euripides' intent is
simply to illustrate an easy lesson in the golden mean. Rather
he seems to be stressing the idea that each of these forces in man
calls for an absolute commitment which will brook no com-
promise, that once the individual yields to either of these needs
of his nature, his will is no longer free to balance and moderate.

It is not possible, I think, to determine whether Euripides
believed that the irrational power which so devastated Phaedra
is to be thought of as springing from her own psyche or from a
universal force in nature. The fact that he has externalized
it in the godhead of Aphrodite suggests that he may have thought
of the sexual drive as being supra-personal. A later play, the
Bacchae, though admittedly its interpretation is debatable, seems
to me to indicate an irrational power which definitely cannot be
explained in terms of human projection (so far as Euripides is
concerned). It would be tempting here to interpret Euripides
as having by poetic intuition anticipated something comparable
to Jung's collective unconscious. This would be to say that each
of us is motivated to greater or less extent by irrational forces
common to us all and stemming from somewhere beyond the
conscious mind. Jung would certainly agree with Euripides
that too great submission to these unconscious forces brings
madness and destruction as happened to Phaedra but that to
deny them and cut oneself off at the roots, so to speak, results
in sterility, emotional starvation, the neurotic lack of any real
contact with humanity which we see portrayed in Hippolytus.

We need not, of course, accept a Jungian type of interpretation. But if we do not, then at least we must realize that Euripides sees the human being as driven by emotional forces which his will power and rational deliberation cannot control. Phaedra herself says this.

> In the long hours of night I have not slept
> for wondering why the life of man goes bad.
> I think that not according to their gifts
> of mind do they decline, since many are wise,
> but one should see it this way: we all know
> the good and see it plain, but will not work
> to have it, some from indolence, and some
> prefer some other pleasure than the one
> of honor.

Euripides is in all probability reacting deliberately against the Socratic dictum that if a man knows what is good, he will choose it. There is no better classical anticipation of Nietzsche's pronouncement to the effect that ethical systems are but the sign language of emotions.

In close relation to this view of the play as the conflict of abstractions symbolized by the deities and incarnated in the mortals, we might also interpret it as a study in *sophrosyne,* the untranslatable Greek word connoting temperance, self-discipline, the golden mean. Often the tragedy has been interpreted in this way, with Phaedra representing the excess by giving too much importance to sex and passion, and Hippolytus the deficiency. If this is the case, then Euripides has certainly introduced several variations on the theme. Phaedra is guilty of excess, to be sure, but not in the obvious sense. So far from being a woman who views adultery lightly, she has chosen to die by starvation rather than reveal her passion. Her final death is not so much due to love as to wounded pride and fear of loss of reputation. Hippolytus, ironically enough, has consciously devoted his whole life to the pursuit of purity and considers himself almost a living personification of *sophrosyne.* His death results less from his refusal to sleep with his stepmother (certainly no real solution) than from his overvehement denunciation of Phaedra, his bitter revelation of disgust and of the feeling that he was defiled by the mere suggestion of any such relation. Thus it was in reality Hippolytus' self-righteous arrogance and Phaedra's pride of reputation which destroyed them rather than either excess or deficiency as related to sexual passion. Is Euripides saying that the true opposite of temperance (*sophrosyne*) is neither sexual license nor asceticism but pride (*hybris*)? One thing is sure: he is hardly taking the conventional view—as is witnessed by Hippolytus' statement when he learns of Phaedra's death.

> She controlled herself
> who had no self-control, and I, who can
> control myself, have done so, to my harm.

Yet when proper recognition has been given to the abstract levels, the fact remains that here, as in almost all his plays, Euripides' principal interest is in the human characters, to whom he has given highly individualized and living personalites. Leave out the goddesses, substitute an assassin's spear for the sea monster, and *Hippolytus* becomes an eminently *human* play with an entirely credible plot, a complex plot which forbids any reduction to a simple conflict between opposing types. Perhaps the greatest tribute to the drama is the fact that it is impossible to pass judgment on the right and wrong of the protagonists without a careful analysis of the total situation from each one's point of view.

Let us look first at Phaedra. Although she is the honored wife of a king who loves her, she has become so through no choice of her own but merely as a prize of war to a victorious invader. Theseus, one would guess, is much older than Phaedra, and he seems to have aroused in her never more than a dutiful respect. That her conscious loyalty is accompanied by hidden hostility one can easily imagine. Nor must we forget her family background. Her mother, Pasiphae, goaded by a mad infatuation for a bull, had given birth to the monstrous Minotaur. An earlier ancestress, Europa, had been carried off by Zeus disguised as a bull and had never been seen again. Phaedra's sister Ariadne had eloped with Theseus; abandoned by him on the island of Naxos, she was made the bride of Dionysus. Phaedra's reference to Pasiphae and Ariadne is of interest. In her conversation with the Nurse she calls upon her mother and sister and refers to herself as making with them a trio of women destroyed by love. Since this immediately precedes her confession of her own guilty passion for Hippolytus, she seems here to be offering her relatives' examples almost as an excuse for herself. There are, I believe, two aspects to this sense of family identity. On the one hand, Phaedra either inherits or thinks that she inherits (which amounts to the same thing) the violent passions of her family. She appears to be giving way to a fatal acceptance of the idea that with such heredity, her passion and destruction are inevitable, that resistance is useless. At the same time her horror at the notoriety of her kinswomen makes her resolve to die rather than be publicly known to be like them.

Thus long before she met Hippolytus, Phaedra must have cherished an ambivalent attitude toward Aphrodite, a horror before those who too easily yielded to sexual attraction, combined with an exaggerated idea of its irresistible power. Even Theseus, since Phaedra was his wife by force of conquest, may have seemed to her one more example of sexual aggression. No wonder she fell in love with Hippolytus. It is not only because he is young and handsome, nor because she is piqued by his indifference to her and to women generally. There are two other, fatal factors. First, Hippolytus' very existence, his "illegitimate" existence, is due to Theseus' having ravished another prize of war, the Amazon Hippolyta. In a sense Phaedra

and Hippolytus are both injured victims of Theseus, even though
his later behavior to them has won at least their willed devotion
and loyalty. Even more important, Hippolytus, by his rejection
of Aphrodite, symbolizes that sexual purity and inviolate in-
tegrity which Phaedra so highly values and perhaps envies.
Illogically she wants to possess it, even though to do so would be
to destroy it. Once she has acknowledged this desire, Phaedra
is wholly obsessed by it. Any hope of coming to terms with
Aphrodite's power is rendered impossible in advance by her
exaggerated fear of it. She must either give in or commit suicide.

In this connection it is important to remember that Euripides
had written an earlier version of the Hippolytus story in which
Phaedra personally offered herself to Hippolytus, and we are
told that the Athenians were so shocked by her that Euripides
decided to rewrite the play.[4] While it is useless to speculate as
to exactly what kind of woman Phaedra was in the lost drama,
it is important not to forget Euripides' original intention.   It
forbids us to adopt any view that Phaedra in the present play is
simply the victim of the Nurse's betrayal. I suspect that in the
earlier production Euripides may have begun the story at a
later stage in the plot, possibly having Phaedra tell of her earlier conflict rather than appearing as she is still struggling with
herself. It seems that our *Hippolytus* must surely be the better
of the two. At least Phaedra's first scene, where Euripides allows
us to see more deeply into her psyche than she herself dares to
do, is one of Euripides' greatest achievements. The later speech
in which Phaedra discusses with the Chorus her earlier attempt
at repression would by itself justify the claim that Euripides
has anticipated not only the modern psychological drama but
even actual tenets of psychoanalysis. Yet I think there has been
a tendency on the part of critics to deal with the whole question
of Phaedra's early silence and later confession in terms over-

---

[4]Augustus Nauck, *Tragicorum Graecorum Fragmenta* (Leipzig: Teubner,
1889), p. 491.

general or physiological. It is true that she has been literally starving herself to death, but I do not think we need to go so far as Grube in saying that her near-delirium and final submission to the Nurse are the result of physical weakness after fasting.[5] Dodds holds that Phaedra exhibits the same characteristics as "most victims of psychological conflict." She tried first to repress the dangerous feelings, and this method inevitably failed. The hidden desire grew stronger, and Phaedra sought symbolic satisfaction in wild flights of fancy where she roamed (obviously with Hippolytus) through the forest and along the seashore. Finally realizing the emptiness of these fantasies, she rationalized her longing to speak—by claiming that the Nurse as suppliant had the right to demand an answer and must be satisfied.[6]

I can only partially agree with Dodds' explanation. Of course Phaedra was unsuccessful in attempting repression, and she was clearly lying to herself when she allowed the Nurse's right as suppliant to outrank all other considerations. But I do not believe that Phaedra's rambling talk represents symbolic assuagement of unconscious desires. Her craving for the virgin spring and for deep sleep in the grassy meadows is undoubtedly symbolic both of her desire for Hippolytus and of longing for coolness and peaceful oblivion as an antidote to her devastating flame of unappeased passion. But there is no hidden symbolism in her desire to hunt in the forest, to watch the race horses, and to break the Venetian colts. Phaedra could not fail to see the company in which she was in imagination carrying on these pursuits. Our only wonder is that the Nurse and the Chorus did not immediately see the connection with Hippolytus, and we can conclude that only the monstrous quality of the suspicion delayed their recognition.

---

[5]G. M. A. Grube, *The Drama of Euripides* (London: Methuen, 1941), p. 180.
[6]E. R. Dodds, "The ΑΙΔΩΣ of Phaedra and the Meaning of the *Hippolytus,*" *Classical Review,* XXXIX (1925), 102-104.

This I hold to be the main point. Phaedra is struggling with two desires. She wants to maintain her reputation un-sullied by concealing her love; at the same time she yearns for the relief which confession would bring. She is the criminal whose whole nature craves to reveal the guilty secret; she is any lover wanting to give expression to an all-consuming pas-sion. Phaedra knows well and later says in so many words that once a secret is first spoken, it is inevitably told abroad. It is unlikely that she would fear that either the Nurse or one of the well-disposed women of Troezen would tell her secret to Theseus. To whom then? Obviously to Hippolytus. Here is the conflict. Phaedra's rational will is resolved on dying rather than giving in to a passion she condemns. But her emotional nature whispers the hope that perhaps if Hippolytus knew . . . . The idea that he might know and respond sympathetically is never mentioned aloud and probably never explicity recognized by Phaedra even inwardly. But it is there in the background, producing the overwhelming compulsion to speak. Phaedra's behavior is that of anyone who feels that to reveal a secret would be unwise or indiscreet—and dangerously exciting.

Phaedra's conflict is waged in bad faith. First of all, she will not admit to herself that fear of betrayal is balanced by a hope of what betrayal might win. Secondly, she plays the game in such a way that she can persuade herself that she has never willingly confessed her love but was compelled by extreme forces. From the beginning her conduct and words are calcu-lated to make further inquiry inevitable. Her resolve to die by fasting (in itself an overreaction) is certain to attract atten-tion. It enables Phaedra to think she has chosen death in prefer-ence to wrongdoing; yet it keeps her alive in case the situation should change. In other words she is not ill as the result of her repressed love; she is making herself ill as a way of expressing her love and in order to be forced to speak it openly. Her delirious words will guide her listeners' attention in the right direction or at least cause them to question further. She forces the Nurse to search desperately for the cause of all of Phaedra's strange behavior and then suddenly admits to a feeling of compulsion to satisfy the Nurse's suppliant inquiry. Even as she admits her love, Phaedra tries to evade the responsibility for having named her lover.

> NURSE   What's that? You are in love, my child?
> With whom?
> PHAEDRA   What do you call him—oh, the Amazon's—
> NURSE   You say Hippolytus?
> PHAEDRA   You say, not I.

The most important question in our interpretation of Phaedra's character hinges on whether or not we think her to have known of the Nurse's true intention in going to Hippolytus. It is my belief that Phaedra did know but in the same way that she knew of her real motive in finally revealing her secret to the Nurse; that is, she refused to admit to herself that the Nurse would betray her, willed not to know it, and forced herself to act as though she did not. Several things bear out this view. When the Nurse, quickly recovering from her outraged shock at the news, tries to persuade Phaedra to yield to love, Phaedra's first fear is not that she will be betrayed but that she will be persuaded.

> Oh, by the gods—for you speak evil well—
> go not beyond this much! I have endured
> to lose my life to love, and that is well,
> but if you plead for evil handsomely,
> I shall be utterly destroyed, reduced
> to that dishonor which I now escape.

Still more obviously, when the Nurse proposes the scheme of the love-charm cure, Phaedra is not really deceived but knows

well that the Nurse's cure for love will be love-satisfied. She
practically says this.

> PHAEDRA   I fear lest I may find you far too wise.
> NURSE   Then anything might scare you! What's this
>   dread?
> PHAEDRA   That you let Theseus' son learn any of this.
> NURSE   Leave that to me. I shall arrange this well.

The Nurse has made no promises; she implicitly admits that
Phaedra's suspicion is correct. Yet Phaedra allows her to go and
is content to let the obvious fiction stand. Later of course
Phaedra reprimands the Nurse but as one reproaches a giver of
bad advice rather than a traitor. The Nurse remarks that if she
had succeeded in her mission, she would have won praise. Phaedra says merely,

> Stop talking! You advised me before this
> not at all well, and what you did you did
> badly. But go now. Get out of the way.

In urging Phaedra's ultimate responsibilty, I do not mean
to suggest that the Nurse is nothing but a dramatic device whereby Phaedra may inform Hippolytus of her guilty passion without offending the Athenian audience. Even if in origin she was
exactly this, Euripides, who was accused by Aristophanes of
giving too much importance to characters of low social position,
has fashioned the Nurse with particular care. She is an interesting person just in herself—half humorous, half pathetic, a
wholly credible mixture of conventionality and earthiness, loyalty and self-pity. Given to garrulous philosophizing on the evils
of earthly existence and the uncertainty of afterlife, she is quick
to grasp for expedient and practical methods of making the
present endurable for those she loves. For years she has been
like a mother to Phaedra; now she is ready to defy even the
most sacred laws to bring her love-sick child forbidden happi-

ness. We cannot completely exempt her from responsibility. On the most favorable reading of events, she is at least conniving with Phaedra. We could even go so far as to say that without the Nurse, Phaedra would probably not have had the courage to take a positive step. Yet neither can we excuse Phaedra on the Nurse's account. We might just as well seek to defend her by saying that she would not have betrayed Theseus if he had never begot a bastard son. That is true, and it is perhaps right that Theseus should share the blame. It is no justification for Phaedra. Euripides' great skill as a dramatist is revealed in precisely this interweaving of responsibilties. Any one of the participants might have prevented the tragedy if he had chosen to act differently; no one of them could have acted other than he did without being inconsistent with what Euripides has shown us of his basic attitudes.

Phaedra's greatest crime, however, is neither her love nor her suicide but her false accusation of Hippolytus. Euripides never seems to condone this act, but he makes it believable and consistent with his earlier sympathetic delineation of Phaedra. It is explained if not justified by the vehemence of Hippolytus' outraged rejection and by his hint that in spite of his oath to keep silent, he may yet reveal the truth to Theseus. Hippolytus' words condemn Phaedra by showing her to be one of the type of women $he has most despised. Her fear of being known to be such had already made her resolve on death. Her resolution now is not made in bad faith but in earnest. The destruction of Hippolytus is partially for the sake of vengeance—and the injury he had inflicted on Phaedra is sufficient in itself to explain her act. It is also to discredit in advance any tale which he may tell of her. She judges correctly that suicide will guarantee her own truthfulness in Theseus' mind. Thus she dies and forges a falsehood so that she may protect what she valued even more highly than life—her reputation. Nor should we forget that this good name involves also that of her children.

In spite of Phaedra's bad faith, her timid fear of others' opinions, her evasion of responsibility for her own acts, her ungovernable passion, her vindictive pride, she remains somehow a sympathetic character. Hippolytus we may finally pardon because we understand him, but Phaedra appeals to us directly. This, I believe, is because her struggle is a real one and against overwhelming odds: a split in her own nature, a shallow confidante who sees only what is superficially expedient, and the trick of circumstance which brought her into contact with the one human being certain to arouse her passion and incapable of understanding it.

The care with which Euripides has worked out the complexities of Phaedra has led at least one critic[7] to consider her the central figure of the tragedy. Apparently Racine and Seneca also found in Phaedra the pivotal character, and it is around her that they have centered the interest of their own plays. I do not believe that Euripides intended his audience to have this reaction. Certainly Phaedra is a heroine in her own right and not merely a foil to Hippolytus. But it is Hippolytus who begins and ends the action and who in the final analysis is even more responsible for what happens than Phaedra. His character has frequently been misunderstood, so much so that later writers using the story have felt it necessary to add motivations which are altogether absent as Euripides has developed the theme. Thus Racine explains Hippolytus' actions by representing him as in love with a girl named Aricie. Robinson Jeffers presents him as homosexual.[8] David Grene explains him as undersexed in the manner of most athletes! There is no justification for any of these views. They hinder rather than aid in interpretation,

---

[7]David Grene, *Three Greek Tragedies in Translation* (Chicago: University of Chicago Press, 1942), pp. 155 ff.

[8]Robinson Jeffers, "The Cretan Woman," contained in *Hungerfield and Other Poems* (New York: Random House, 1951).

and one wonders why these authors felt it necessary to invent where Euripides is really so clear and so satisfactory.

It seems to me wholly impossible to find in Hippolytus simply a shy adolescent, though it has been suggested that he is such.[9] Moreover, we are doing an injustice to Euripides if we try to make Hippolytus an innocent victim by pointing out that he had no other alternative. It is true that it would have been no solution if he had slept with his father's wife. This would merely have resulted in a different type of tragedy. But Hippolytus does more than submit. He acts. His vehement rejection and denunciation of Phaedra, the particular nature of his interview with Theseus, and the remarks made by both father and son are proof that Euripides regarded the plot as the inevitable outcome of the interlocking of three complex personalities, not the study of the effect of one woman's passion on two people who happened to be its recipient and victim.

From the beginning of the play Euripides takes care to underscore the abnormal character of Hippolytus' attitude. Aphrodite points out at the start that his scorn of her is beyond all reason. Theseus taunts him with boasting overmuch of his purity and implies that Hippolytus is a member of a fanatically ascetic religious group. Hippolytus himself indicates a more than normal aversion to women in two places: First there is the speech to the Nurse in which, before reproaching Phaedra specifically, he violently attacks all women and goes so far as to wish that men might dispense with the female entirely and obtain offspring by depositing money for them at a temple. I

---

[9]See André-Jean Festugière, *Personal Religion among the Greeks* (Berkeley: University of California Press, 1954), pp. 11 ff. Festugière develops the view that Hippolytus is imbued with mystic piety but denies that there is in him any kind of abnormality or unhealthy exaggeration. Somewhat the same interpretation is given by Louis Méridier, who extends the idea so as to picture Hippolytus winning divinity through his renunciation of the flesh and his subsequent martyrdom. For Méridier's very detailed analysis, see his *Hippolyte d'Euripide. Etude et analyse* (Paris: Librairie Mellottée, 1931).

am sure that this preposterous substitution of a temple for the
marriage bed and childbirth is not primarily humorous and not
accidental on Euripides' part. It represents Hippolytus' serious
wish that the purity of a spiritual conception and birth could
replace what is to him the earthy and unclean sexual aspect.
Again in the speech to Theseus Hippolytus' defense is based
largely on an appeal to his well-known virginity. Not only has
he never known a woman sexually; he has not even been interested in looking at his companions' prize sets of pornographic
drawings!

If then we accept the idea that Hippolytus' attitude toward
women and sex was not normal, what was its cause and origin?

In his portrayal of Hippolytus as in that of Phaedra Euripides shows himself concerned with family connections. We
are several times reminded that Hippolytus is not Theseus' lawful heir but an illegitimate son by Hippolyta. Thus from one
point of view Hippolytus forms a parallel to the bastard
Edmund in Shakespeare's *King Lear*. Although in the case of
Hippolytus the son has outwardly felt only affectionate loyalty
to his father, the presence of long-unexpressed resentment comes
out even at the moment when he is forgiving Theseus. Hippolytus' dying words, "Pray to have lawful sons as true as I," certainly parallel the brief dialogue which takes place at the time
of Edmund's death.

> EDGAR   The gods are just, and of our pleasant vices
> Make instruments to scourge us.
> EDMUND   Th' hast spoken right; tis true.
> The wheel is come full circle. I am here.

Hippolytus has evidently flaunted his life of sexual abstinence,
vegetarianism, and so forth to the point where Theseus has been
considerably irritated. Possibly the motive for this public dis-
play of purity on Hippolytus' part was precisely that he might
serve as a living reproach to Theseus. Be this as it may, it seems

very probable that one reason for Hippolytus' disgust with everything pertaining to sex stems from his embarrassment over his illegitimacy. Euripides makes it quite clear that Phaedra's children will be preferred as heirs before him. Though Hippolytus shows no signs of being unduly ambitious, his inferior status may well have rankled.

Along with this "social motivation" there is something deeper and stronger. This is the influence of the ravished Hippolyta, his mother. Here as with Phaedra Euripides seems to be stressing ancestry both as an actual hereditary factor and as psychological motivation. The cult of sexual purity—or sexual abnormality, as one may choose to call it—belonged as much to Hippolyta the Amazon as to her son. We may say that he inherited her lack of emotional balance or that he perpetuated it either in filial, loving remembrance or in revolt at her outrage. The worship of Artemis too he got from Hippolyta, another devotee, and this is important in more than the obvious sense: in itself, of course, it indicates that Hippolytus is in a manner identifying himself with his mother. Even more he is worshiping his mother. Artemis is a substitute for Hippolyta, the chaste maiden huntress, the woman so adept at masculine pursuits that Hippolytus can denounce womankind as a whole without in his own mind including her. Thus the dominance of Artemis in Hippolytus' life is also the dominance of his own mother-ideal. Against an emotional background such as this it is easy to see how he would be abnormally outraged by Phaedra's passion. Already resented by Hippolytus for having usurped Hippolyta's position, Phaedra as Theseus' wife symbolically stands as well for Hippolytus' own mother, so that sinning with her would be incest as well as betrayal. Hippolytus' behavior with regard to Phaedra as with women in general follows the familiar pattern of the Oedipus complex. The question will be raised as to how much of this Euripides had in mind. As much probably as Sophocles had when writing *Oedipus Tyrannus*.

Poets have intuited since long before psychologists began to formulate.

We cannot, however, dismiss Hippolytus with so relatively simple a classification. His is a complicated character and one which seems at first to be shot through with contradictions. On the one hand he appears to be guided wholly by emotion. His devotion to Artemis is of an intense, almost fanatical sort. Theseus' reference to his vegetarian practices suggests that he was also an Orphic, a member of a cult notorious for mingling asceticism and pursuit of ecstatic union with the divine. Theseus says,

> Go peddle your pure food
> of vegetables lacking little souls!
> Take Orpheus for your master, revel in
> rare esctasies and treasure up the fumes
> of many scriptures!

At the same time Theseus accuses him of sophistry, and it is true that Hippolytus, though not guilty, reasons less like a man totally absorbed in proving his innocence than in the manner of a self-conscious intellectual trying to prove a point. One might be tempted to dismiss this fact since, as Aristophanes pointed out, Euripides has a tendency to represent all of his characters as trained in Sophistic debating. But there is at least one other passage which points to this same kind of intellectual detachment on the part of Hippolytus. In his first shocked reaction to Theseus' accusation he says,

> If I could only stand there opposite
> and look upon myself, so I might weep
> to see what great injustice I endure!

Theseus' answer to this exclamation is scathing and penetrating and at least partially correct.

> Indeed your discipline has rather been
> rapt worship of yourself than to fulfill
> the pieties due your parents, and be just.

To which Hippolytus in turn replies,

> Oh, my poor mother! Oh, that bitter birth!
> May none I care for have a bastard's life!

In this passage I think we have the clue to what is the core of Hippolytus' trouble—a narcissism stemming from deep-set emotional maladjustment. Theseus' statement is only partly true. On the surface Hippolytus is eminently and unpleasantly self-centered. His prudish self-righteousness forbids any attempt to understand or sympathize with Phaedra. His boasts of perfect purity are nauseating to the spectator as well as to Theseus. His statement that he was timid in a crowd and got along only with a select coterie betrays aristocratic arrogance. Worse than all of these traits, there is downright sadism in his statement to the Nurse that he will come back when Theseus returns and will enjoy watching Phaedra's guilt-conscious conduct. Yet in all of these reactions we may read the behavior of the unhappy neurotic so preoccupied with his own maladjustment that he is utterly incapable of forming normal human relationships. There is perhaps as much of self-hate as of self-love in this egocentrism. In fact Hippolytus' refusal to save himself by the oath which his intellect had already refused to accept as binding is almost masochistic, coming close to being a self-inflicted martyrdom— as though inwardly he recognizes his guilty failure to produce any outgoing emotion toward anyone.

Finally we should briefly consider Theseus. Certainly he as well as Phaedra is responsible for Hippolytus' death; and, as Hippolytus points out in the final scene, Theseus is the one whose loss is greatest even though he alone is still to live. Theseus is not as complicated as either of the other principals;

in fact he comes close to functioning as the one wholly normal character against whom the psychological distortions of Phaedra and Hippolytus may be measured. Yet though he strikes us as behaving exactly as one would expect a man in his position to behave, Theseus is not a type character. He is evidently a man capable of deep affection but without true understanding or sensitive perception. His lament over Phaedra's death is sincere and expressed with an intense lyricism which we find nowhere else in his speeches. Later he is incapable of unmitigated satisfaction when he learns that the son he still believes disloyal is dying. But he has completely failed to notice that Phaedra was in any way troubled. He had evidently long been irritated by Hippolytus' way of life but without ever trying to come to a real understanding with him. When he discovers Phaedra's suicide, he is so lacking in any sort of wisdom stemming from either introspection or observation of others that he can find recourse only in the theory of ancestral predestination and family curse.

> And what is to blame,
> if not some far-off long-forgot ancestral crime
> that, guided by the powers above,
> has overtaken me in later time?[10]

This is no soul-examining fear of the consequences of sin but rather a mere superstition of the sort expressed later when he anxiously begs Hippolytus to free him from the stain of bloodguilt.

Theseus displays an interesting mixture of rationalism and

---

[10]Hippolytus says almost the same thing when he is brought in after the accident, just before his reconciliation with Theseus. I am tempted to see in this filial echo evidence that Hippolytus, despite his proud independence, has been profoundly influenced by the father toward whom he cherishes strongly ambivalent feelings. We are on safer ground perhaps in concluding simply that Euripides underscores here Hippolytus' complete inability to acknowledge his own part in precipitating Phaedra's death and lies.

distrust of reason which may not be wholly consistent but which was probably fairly typical of the average Athenian. His only direct appeal to divinity is his prayer to Poseidon when he asks the god to accomplish an act of vengeance which he cannot bring himself to perform with his own hand. Theseus' faith in Poseidon's promise is hardly that which moves mountains. In fact he feels it necessary to add the more tangible curse of banishment to insure that at least something will be accomplished. His appraisal of possibilities is almost a Hellenic equivalent of Pascal's wager—except that Theseus better defends himself against the negative eventuality.

> I banish him
> out of this land, so that of two fates one
> at least will strike him. Either Poseidon will
> honor my curses, kill him, send him down
> into the gates of Hades, or, cast out
> from Troezen, and a vagabond, he shall
> in strange lands drain a thin life to the dregs!

When it comes to really important decisions, Theseus chooses the reasonable use of evidence in preference to religious signs sent by Heaven. Hippolytus would like to attest his innocence by consultation with priests and soothsayers.

HIPPOLYTUS Will you discount all pledges, oaths,
and signs
read by the priests, and banish me untried?
THESEUS This tablet, though no prophet has subscribed
an omen to it, still accuses you
with perfect certainty. And to your birds
wandering overhead I say fare you well!

The rationalism which Theseus here professes must not be confused with philosophical reasoning. When Hippolytus defends himself in a carefully organized speech, appealing to his father's sense of logic in the situation, Theseus sneers at him.

> Is this man not a born singer of spells,
> a vocal wizard, who thinks he can rule
> my heart with his bland equanimity,
> after dishonoring his father so!

Theseus will not give the name of reason to the Sophists' formal persuasion. Elsewhere he wistfully expresses the futility of the human mind, which has developed all sorts of skills but which cannot teach true wisdom to the foolish or distinguish the true from the false.

> Mankind! Your utmost efforts are in vain!
> Why do you teach ten thousand kinds of skill,
> invent all things, discover everything,
> when you have never learned nor hunted out
> a way to teach the mindless how to think?

There is a suggestion throughout the play that Theseus is too busy being a king (probably a very good king) and a man of action for him to think deeply of the people about him or of his relation to them. His reaction to Phaedra's letter is inevitable. The circumstances seem to accuse Hippolytus in such a way as to leave no possible doubt of his guilt. Theseus would not be one to imagine that a woman would kill herself to support a false accusation, and he is conventional enough to accept the alleged cause as adequate. The fact that Hippolytus remarks that he had just left Phaedra alive piles up the circumstantial evidence. If Theseus had been judging a case in which he himself was not involved, he might perhaps have examined more closely the arguments offered by Hippolytus. The Athenian courts were far more disposed than those of today to decide a man's guilt or innocence on the basis of whether or not his over-all "character" was consistent with the act of which he was accused. But Theseus is not without prejudice where Hippolytus is concerned. Hippolytus' chief defense, his too-much-vaunted purity, has already been a source of irritation to Theseus. The temptation to conclude that it was a false front all along is too strong.

We must pronounce Theseus technically guilty and fully responsible for the denouement both because he is paying the penalty for his earlier act of violence against Hippolyta and— more specifically—because he proclaims the death curse on the basis of superficial appearances, acts too quickly and without investigating the situation carefully or really listening to the defense offered by Hippolytus or to the words of the Chorus. Yet if we look more deeply, we feel that Theseus could not have done otherwise, that he too has allowed himself to be governed by emotional forces too powerful to permit his usual deliberation to enter in.

I have discussed *Hippolytus* as a drama of character, which I believe it to be. I do not think that tiny loopholes in the plot are sufficient to put the play even slightly into the realm of a tragedy of fate. As I indicated earlier, the Nurse's betrayal of Phaedra is not really unexpected by her mistress, and it could have been forestalled. Thus it does not clear Phaedra of responsibility. Again, it seems to me that Theseus' curse is as definitely a method of killing Hippolytus as a thrust of the sword would have been. Certainly this is the way in which Artemis takes it later.

Much has been made of the point that if Theseus had really believed in the power of his wish, he would not have bothered with the decree of exile and that hence he did not inwardly wish to destroy Hippolytus completely.[11] Such an argument seems to me to be mere quibbling. Insufficient time has elapsed between the pronouncement of the curse and the banishment

---

[11]Gilbert Norwood, *Essays on Euripidean Drama* (Berkeley: University of California Press, 1954), p. 87.

for us to postulate any seeming indication to Theseus that the wish will not be granted. Meanwhile what is he to do? He will hardly keep Hippolytus there before his eyes while he awaits the outcome. Furthermore when the news of the sea-bull's attack on Hippolytus is brought to him, Theseus shows no sign either of surprise or of repentance.

Finally, what we are to make of the fact that neither Hippolytus nor the Chorus tells Theseus the truth when he believes Phaedra's lying accusation? This, I believe, is the weakest point in the play. Obviously if the truth had been proved to Theseus, the tragedy would have ended right then. So far as Hippolytus is concerned, there is no real difficulty. I have already suggested one reason for his silence. Religious scruples (since he *was* after all a religious fanatic) might well be sufficient answer. Furthermore, Hippolytus himself points out that if he did tell the truth, Theseus would not believe him. The silence of the Chorus is a more serious problem, for it seems that Theseus would have had to be convinced by the group of women if they had done more than to insist with no explanation that Hippolytus was not guilty. We may, of course, point to the fact that the Chorus also had promised not to betray Phaedra. I suspect that Euripides considered the oath sufficient to justify their not speaking. To me this hardly seems convincing since the vow was made before the women knew Phaedra's intention. It is possible that we should consider the use of the three oaths—Hippolytus', the Chorus', and Poseidon's—as a direct attack by Euripides on the practice of thus following the letter rather than the spirit of a sacred promise or of letting a minor religious scruple stand in the way of true justice. Otherwise I suspect we must acknowledge here that Euripides did not quite overcome the limitations imposed by the convention of keeping the Chorus always on the stage. The difficulty, however, is not vital, for even without the whole truth, Theseus could have refrained from immediate action. To what the Chorus does say, he pays no attention whatsoever.

Evidently Euripides intended to present a tragedy which on one level may be read as stemming wholly from the emotional involvement of three human beings, portrayed for us with a psychological insight unparalleled in Greek drama. That the personality of each one hastened on the tragic denouement appears beyond dispute. Euripides evidently believed that our rational natures do not wholly determine our acts. The larger question as to whether, from some eternal perspective, a person must be held to be fully responsible for his total personality and consequently for his final decisions is one for which I do not believe that Euripides as a philosopher ever quite found a satisfactory answer. As a dramatist, however, he resolved the problem by so clearly analyzing the inner life of his characters that we can experience the events from each one's point of view. Such understanding necessarily induces sympathy.

THE MYTH

No study of *Hippolytus* would be complete without some consideration of the myth on which Euripides has based his play. Apparently the relation of the unhappy principals has undergone no significant change at the dramatist's hand, though there may have been some alteration of chronology. It is probable, for example, that in his earlier tragedy Euripides allowed Phaedra to remain alive until after she had personally accused Hippolytus and effected his death, and we cannot say whether this version was closer to or farther from the myth as commonly told in Athens.

It has been customary for scholars to try to connect this story with that of Joseph and Potiphar's wife and with the Egyptian "Tale of Two Brothers," implying a common origin. While this kind of assertion can never be disproved, it seems to me both improbable and unnecessary. To begin with, the three tales are unlike in every respect save for the fact that the heroine for mingled motives of self-protection and vengeance falsely accuses the object of her unreciprocated passion. In neither of the non-Greek narratives does the woman kill herself; in neither is the relation involved that of stepmother and stepson. The dissimilarities are far greater than the one likeness, and there is certainly no way of proving influence. Given any society whatsoever in which a woman would incur reproach for unreciprocated advances and be blamed for infidelity to her husand, this kind of story is almost inevitable. Under less dramatic circumstances women and men are every day claiming to have rebuffed when in reality they have been rejected. We are dealing with a plot only slightly less universally human than the fatal triangle itself.

When we look at other Greek references to the myth, we find that Euripides has made one important omission. He has said nothing about Hippolytus' being resurrected. The pre-Euripidean version of the myth included a resurrection of the hero; there are references to it made by the author of the *Carmen Naupactium*, an epic poem of uncertain date but evidently written before the fifth century B.C., probably before the sixth. Fragments of this poem state that Asclepius restored Hippolytus to life and was blasted by a thunderbolt for so doing.[1] That this conclusion to the story was well known is supported by the fact that the Romans (and possibly earlier colonists from Troezen) used it as a means of connecting Hippolytus with a local Italian deity, Virbius, who was worshiped at Aricia near or in a sanctuary of Diana. Virgil gives us the fullest account of this association. He says that Artemis after Hippolytus' death persuaded Asclepius to bring him to life again. She then transported Hippolytus to her grove at Aricia where he married the goddess Egeria and lived on apparently forever. Some of the ancient writers said that Artemis henceforth called him Virbius, which the Romans took to mean twice a man (*vir* plus *bis*), hence twice born. Virgil, however, says that Virbius was the son of Hippolytus. Owing to the manner of Hippolytus' earlier death, the grove was forbidden to horses![2] This late Roman account would, of course, be of no use to us by itself; combined with the early quotation from the *Carmen Naupactium*, it is signifi-

---

[1] Godofredus Kinkel, *Epicorum Graecorum Fragmenta* (Leipzig: Teubner, 1877), Vol. I, p. 202.

[2] Virgil, *Aenead* vii, lines 775 ff. Ovid, *Fasti* v, lines 312 ff. and *Metamorphoses* xv, lines 545 ff. Strabo iii, 263 ff. Pausanias, *Corinth* xxvii, 4.

cant as indicating the common prevalence of an aspect of the myth which Euripides has ignored.

It is not difficult to see why Euripides disregarded this conclusion to the myth. To prophesy resurrection and divinity for Hippolytus would destroy the tragic effect and dull the edge of Euripides' criticism of the Olympians. Furthermore, the Hippolytus created by Euripides is utterly unsuited to the role of a martyred mortal earning the status of deity through heroic exploits. Artemis tells us, to be sure, that the girls on the eve of their weddings will place locks of hair on his grave, will sing choruses of mourning for him and will celebrate Phaedra's unhappy passion (an odd way of pleasing him, I should think). But as Euripides handles this prophecy, it takes on the character of a memorial honor for a mortal. Any divinity on Hippolytus' part is played down if not wholly suppressed.

Yet Euripides knew, as we know, that Hippolytus was worshiped as a sacred hero if not a full-scale god. This fact is vital to us if we try to see how the myth arose and what it may have meant before the human love story became predominant. The evidence for Hippolytus' worship is scanty, but it exists and is definite enough. Pausanias in the second century A.D. described a sepulchral monument to Hippolytus which stood on the Athenian Acropolis in front of the temple to Themis. He tells us also of the foundation by Theseus of a cult to Aphrodite Pandemos (Aphrodite of all the people), and implies the existence here of a shrine and images. He refers apparently to the sanctuary of Aphrodite Ἱππολύτῳ δ' ἔπι, which means literally Aphrodite *over* Hippolytus, but which Euripides interprets "for the sake of Hippolytus," saying that Phaedra established it after first falling in love with her stepson.[3] In Laconia also, says Pausanias, there was a hero shrine to Hippolytus. It stood near a sanctuary

---

[3]Pausanias, *Attica* xxii, 1-3. For discussion of the evidence for such a sanctuary see Jane Harrison, *Prolegomena to the Study of Greek Religion* (Cambridge: Cambridge University Press, 1908), pp. 352-354.

of the Great Mother.⁴ The real center of Hippolytus' worship was at Troezen. Here, according to Pausanias, there was a sacred precinct in which stood a temple to Hippolytus with a priest appointed for life to serve Hippolytus with annual sacrifices. The temple contained an old image said to have been made by Diomedes. It was here that the maidens offered up the locks of hair on the eve of their wedding days. Nearby was a temple to Aphrodite Kataskopia (Aphrodite the Spy) where people said Phaedra once spied on Hippolytus as he exercised. One is reminded at this point of some of the present-day stories told by guides to tourists. The impression is strengthened by Pausanias' last bit of information to the effect that near the temple there was a myrtle tree with its leaves pierced with holes, this being the result of Phaedra's attempt to relieve her unsatisfied passion by pricking the leaves with a hairpin!⁵

Though Pausanias is writing in the second century A.D. when the Euripides play itself may well have inspired the legends, he strongly emphasizes the ancient origin of the religious practices. The beginning of the Acropolis worship is attributed to the far past under Theseus, and the statue at Troezen is described as primitive. He reports one other fact of interest. The people of Troezen, he says, "will not have it that he [Hippolytus] was dragged to death by his horses, and though they know his grave they do not show it. But they believe that what is called the Charioteer in the sky is the Hippolytus of the legend, such being the honour he enjoys from the gods."⁶

So much for the rites and worship. What of the myth itself?

Owing to the almost total lack of conclusive evidence, the problem of the origin and primitive meaning of Greek myth has long served as a sort of safety valve for the usually disciplined imagination of classical scholars. Of all the myths,

---

⁴Pausanias, *Laconia* xii, 9.
⁵Pausanias, *Corinth* xxxii, 1-3.
⁶*Idem.*

that of Hippolytus seems most often to have provided a romantic escape from sober reflection. I shall mention only a few of the more lurid theories.

The nineteenth-century writers tended to view all myths as portrayals of natural phenomena. Thus Hippolytus was made a parallel to Phaethon, the son of Apollo, and became a symbol of the sun. His death, caused by the bull from the sea, indicated the setting of the sun at the horizon where sky meets the ocean, or perhaps the eternal conflict of water and fire. Or again, Hippolytus was the morning star, his mother the moon-goddess. Since Phaedra (whose name may mean "the shining one") was made the dawn-goddess, her arrival naturally drove away Hippolyta (as the moon-goddess) and heralded Hippolytus' demise.[7]

Another explanation was based on the apparent etymology of Hippolytus' name. Taking this to mean "loosened by horses," Reinach tried to relate the myth to a primitive ritual in which a sacred horse was torn apart and eaten by his worshipers. The latter, because they were believed to become in this way united with the god, were themselves called horses. Gradually, claimed Reinach, the horse was humanized into a divine hero and the rite transformed into a tale of private calamity. Although the rending and communal eating of a horse may very likely have been a religious practice in Greece at an early period, there seems to be every reason to reject Reinach's theory as applied to Hippolytus. In the first place, names compounded with "hippos" were common enough among Greeks of all periods so that this one instance hardly seems to need elaborate explanation. Moreover, if we are to explain it, it could just as well mean "he of the loosened horse" or "the fast driver." And what, if Reinach is correct, are we to make of Hippolyta—unless she was a mare who for some reason escaped rending in the later

_____
[7]Paul Decharme, *Mythologie de la Grèce antique* (Paris: Garnier, 1886), p. 558.

story? Still more important, there is nothing whatsoever in the known ritual surrounding Hippolytus which in any sense suggests horses—save for the late tabu arising at Aricia. He is said to have presented Asclepius with twenty horses as a token of his appreciation at being restored to life by the god-physician, but this statement is merely consistent with the general tradition that Hippolytus was an athlete and hunter. Finally, what on earth are Phaedra, Theseus, Aphrodite, and Artemis doing in the tale?[8]

L. R. Farnell came a little closer to what appears to me the probable explanation in suggesting that Hippolytus was a priest-attendant on a goddess (Artemis-Aphrodite or Phaedra) and vowed to chastity during his tenure of office. But Farnell weakens his theory, in my opinion, by assuming that the story of a woman's unrequited passion and her subsequent destruction of the priest may refer to an actual event; for he leaves this suggestion suspended in mid-air with no hypothesis as to its connection with Theseus or with Hippolyta. Even worse, he explains Phaedra's suicide by a far-fetched analogy with a "hanging goddess," a personification of the puppets hung on trees in fertility rites.

The most recent hypothesis, by Robert Graves, is utterly disappointing. Graves has made no attempt to treat the myth as a whole or to show how the various personages were brought together. Phaedra he relates, without explanation, to a South Palestinian goddess appearing in inscriptions as Pdri. He claims that she is merely a reduplication of her mother, the Cretan Pasiphae, who was, he says, a moon-goddess. The fatal one-sided love affair he derives either from the Egyptian "Tale of Two Brothers" or a lost Caananite story. The death of Hip-

---

[8]Salomon Reinach, *Cultes, mythes, et religions* (Paris: Leroux, 1913), pp. 54-67. Lewis Richard Farnell criticizes an earlier presentation of this theory by Reinach and presents his own view in *Greek Hero Cults and Ideas of Immortality* (Oxford: Clarendon Press, 1921), pp. 64-70. See also p. 31.

polytus is for Graves one of the many myths going back to a time when the pre-Hellenic sacred king was torn to death by women disguised as mares. In Hellenic times, he maintains, the ritual was changed to replace the women by a four-horse chariot. The entire ceremony, Graves suggests, may be of common origin with a Babylonian ritual in which an interrex is king for a day and then destroyed as the original king is reinstated. Graves' breadth of reading cannot be denied, but one wishes it had been subjected to more of synthesizing reflection.[9]

In view of such contradictory and flamboyant theories as these, one may well hesitate between the fear of being equally reprehensible and the consoling hope that at this point *no* theory is too extreme for publication. Needless to say, the latter is the more attractive alternative, and I should like to present one more hypothesis, in part original and in part based on ideas already worked out by others. I make no claim that the evidence which I offer is conclusive. Unless archaeologists in the future should turn up information more precise than historians of the twilight period of Greek religion have ever dared to hope for, any account of the making of a myth remains even at best a scholarly speculation. Yet in this field of learning as in all others, probability is better than sheer idiocy, and an unproved possibility may be closer to the truth—even if it doesn't quite hit it—than the complacent statement that in uncertain matters we know absolutely nothing.

It seems to me that two aspects of this myth have been slighted in the scholars' interpretations. First, the relation of Hippolytus and Hippolyta has been given too little importance; second, one tends to forget the fact that in the final analysis it is Theseus, not Aphrodite, who is the *direct* cause of Hippolytus' death. Beginning with Hippolyta, we should note the odd fact that Hippolytus, strictly speaking, does not have a

---

[9]Robert Graves, *The Greek Myths* (Baltimore: Penguin, 1955), Section 101, "Phaedra and Hippolytus." See especially pp. 232, 306, and 359.

name of his own but merely the masculine form of his mother's name. This situation is not usual either in ordinary Greek practice or in Greek mythology. Both heroes and gods are frequently referred to as the son or grandson of so-and-so, but this is merely to add a title to the man's own name. Furthermore, the name "Hippolytus" ('Ἱππόλυτος) is not a patronymic, or in this case a matronymic. It could never grammatically be anything other than the masculine form of "Hippolyta" ('Ἱππολύτη). There is no evidence that it was customary at any time in Greek history or even in a pre-Greek matriarchy for a man to be known by his mother's name. The practice is almost unknown elsewhere in Greek mythology.[10] Therefore it seems to me extremely probable that Hippolytus to begin with was not the son of Hippolyta but rather the masculine counterpart of whatever she originally represented. One could, of course, try to invert the relation and see in Hippolyta the feminine aspect of Hippolytus. But such a view appears to be forbidden by the curiously passive role which is ascribed to Hippolytus. He is always subordinate to, frequently the victim of, the acts of others, never the instigator of action. The only positive steps which he does take, his rebuff of Aphrodite and of Phaedra, are

---

[10]I admit that I have not traced down every name available in the records of Greek mythology. Actually the one exception I have encountered is one which suggests that if we knew more about it, there might be still more evidence in support of the hypothesis which I am presenting. Medea, Theseus' hostile stepmother who had to flee Athens after the discovery of her plot to kill Theseus, had a son named Medus (sometimes spelled Medeius). Clearly Medea herself is one of the many matriarchal heroines who are in one way or another overcome by Theseus in the various myths concerning him. In the story of Medea and her son there is one particularly interesting episode. When Medus was held prisoner by his uncle Perses, ruler of Colchis, Medea came to rescue him, *disguising herself as a priestess of Artemis*. It is possible that the Medea-Medus relation was an exact counterpart of that which I am about to suggest for Hippolytus and Hippolyta and that the original connection with Artemis was the same in each case. (For a list of sources for the Medus myth see J. Lemprière, *Classical Dictionary*, New Edition by F. A. Wright [New York: E. P. Dutton, 1951], *s. v.*)

performed largely in the name of a previous commitment, his exclusive devotion to Artemis. Thus we are referred back to Hippolyta, of whom Hippolytus seems to be a reduplication.

Who then was Hippolyta? We are told that she was one of the Amazons, perhaps their queen. Now the Amazons have been called moon-goddesses, have been equated with the Hittites or more generally with any near-East or Pelasgian matriarchal society. One thing seems sure, namely, that they derive from a culture older than that of the Indo-European Hellenes in Greece. This might be inferred in general from their matriarchal character and from the fact that so many of the Greek heroes are represented as coming into conflict with them. The Amazons were believed to be followers of the god Ares, hence warlike, and devotees of Artemis. It was said that their community was made up entirely of women, that they kept the race going either by kidnapping baby girls or by raiding a village and staying there just long enough to conceive children by the male inhabitants. (They kept only the girl babies and either killed the boys or left them with their fathers.)

The most unlikely tale told of these strange women claimed that they cut or burned off one breast in order better to be able to manage javelins and the bow. Ridiculous as this explanation obviously is, the tradition of the one-breasted Amazon was firmly implanted among the Greeks as numerous examples of Greek sculpture bear witness. Modern scholars have been inclined chiefly to dismiss the whole story as the result of a rather late etymological interpretation of "Amazons" as stemming from a-mazos (α-μαζός) or "without a breast." But perhaps this really was the meaning of the word. And if so, why was it applied?

Axel W. Persson in *The Religion of Greece in Prehistoric Times* accepts the derivation, gives evidence to support a pre-Greek tradition of Amazons with one breast, and presents what seems to me a convincing theory regarding the actual practice of such mutilation. Persson's conclusions are based in part on

his study of two rings found at Mycenae. On one we have three
people approaching a sacred shrine. The worshipers are men
wearing women's skirts. About this fact I think there can be no
question. The Mycenaean artists knew well enough how to present the female form, and for these figures there is not only a
definite lack of any bosom but a heavy emphasis on the muscular
development of arms and shoulders. The shrine is marked by
the "horns of consecration" always associated with the Minoan
religion, which centered around an earth-mother or vegetation
goddess. Behind the three men is an insect, probably a bee,
which even in later times seems to have been a sexual symbol.[11]
Persson appears to be on solid ground in concluding that in this
ring we have the primitive equivalent, if not the actual proto-
types, of the later Galli, the eunuch priests of the Earth-Mother
goddess, Kybele.[12]

---

[11]Axel W. Persson, *The Religion of Greece in Prehistoric Times* (Berkeley:
University of California Press, 1942), pp. 56-58 and 89-90. For a provocative
discussion of the bee in connection with Artemis see William Ramsay, *Asianic*
Elements in Greek Civilization (London: J. Murray, 1928), pp. 82 ff. I myself cannot agree with Ramsay's statement that the supposed breasts on the
statues of the Ephesian Artemis are in reality the Queen-bee's ovary and ova. If
this were so, however, it would not undermine Persson's theory. It would
actually strengthen his idea that the men on the ring are early examples of Galli.
With regard to the Amazons discussed in the next paragraph, Ramsay's interpretation would, of course, not support Persson's view in entirety. Yet it would
not destroy it either, especially since by Ramsay's own admission the Greeks at
least *thought* the swellings to be breasts.

[12]Martin Nilsson remarks without any discussion that he does not agree with
Persson's identification of the figures as eunuchs. He believes that they are
women worshipers. I can only say here that when I saw the ring in the National
Museum at Athens, I felt that Persson was right. Nilsson does not comment
on Persson's description of the second ring which I discuss but refers to these
figures too as merely "female." Although the hypothesis that the Amazons (like
the eunuchs) were once attendants on the mother-goddess in Greece would be
weaker without the rings as supporting evidence, my speculation as to the original origin of Hippolyta and Hippolytus would not be seriously affected. See
Nilsson, *The Minoan-Mycenaean Religion and Its Survival in Greek Religion*
(Lund: Gleerup, 1950), pp. 181-182.

The second ring shows a similar shrine, and again there are three worshipers. This time the figures are unmistakably women, but in each case the woman has been portrayed with only one breast. The question now arises as to whether the women pictured here on the ring can be related to rites or personages of a later religion in the same way that the men in skirts may be said to foreshadow the Galli. Persson offers a combination of brilliant insight and sound reasoning to show that such an analogy can be drawn.

At this point we must remind ourselves that Artemis was not in classical times solely the virgin goddess of the hunt and (somewhat contradictorily) the protectress of the wild things of the forest. Her association with childbirth is well known even on the Greek mainland and points to her origin as an early vegetation and fertility goddess. Apparently in the Greek tradition the sexual aspect in her nature was suppressed, perhaps transferred to Aphrodite, and Artemis became the maiden-goddess almost—though never quite—as completely as Athena herself. In Asia Minor, the opposite occurred. The other side of Artemis was developed until she became the fertile mother-goddess *par excellence.* At Ephesus in particular she was as fully a fertility goddess as Kybele and was frequently represented in statues as a woman with many pendulous breasts. Persson refers us to this Ephesian Artemis and points out that in antiquity there was a strong tradition that the one-breasted Amazons had lived near her temple and were intimately associated with her. He points out that, according to the Alexandrian Callimachus, even before the temple of Artemis existed in Ephesus the Amazons had worshiped the goddess in the form of a sacred tree. Classical coins have preserved the tradition of such a tree-goddess, who apparently at Gortyn on Crete was associated with the birth of the young Zeus.[13] All authorities agree that she goes back to the Minoan period.

---

[13]Persson, *op. cit.,* p. 144.

We can see Persson's inevitable conclusion. There is evidence for a fertility goddess worshiped by men who have voluntarily become eunuchs; that is, they have sacrificed their own fertility as the final act of devotion to the fertility goddess. Associated with the same deity are women who have cut off one breast. Surely the act must have paralleled that of the men. Persson says, "The amputation of the Amazon's breast is an act of exactly the same character, a counterpart to male emasculation. In my view, this practice is the real explanation of the many stories about this peculiarly female group in the literature of antiquity." He goes on a bit later to say, "That which the devoted worshipers offer to the goddess for the strengthening of her creative powers is, in turn, visibly expressed in the image of the goddess. The women have brought their offering, as the men theirs." It is Persson's belief that even for the pre-Greek period we have indication that both priests and priestesses served as attendants to a mother-goddess and that the priestesses became in mythology the Amazons.[14]

Persson's theory, if correct, and I believe that it is, would help clear up several puzzling points concerning the Hippolytus myth. Since Hippolytus was a local deity or hero worshiped at Troezen, in all probability before Theseus, it has always seemed to me hard to account for his connection with Hippolyta, who as an Amazon living in Asia Minor could only be brought to Athens by a mythical invasion and battle involving Theseus. But if we accept the evidence of the rings from Mycenae, then the Amazons were in the Peloponnesus before the Greeks and were only removed by legend when the partriarchal had overcome the matriarchal societies of the Greek mainland and—incidentally— when the particular Artemis with whom they were associated existed no longer save in Asia Minor.[15]

---

[14]*Ibid.*, pp. 90 and 145.

[15]I have made no attempt to explain the origin of the name "Hippolyta." I do not think an explanation is necessary here any more than for the many other

This conclusion would aid us too in solving the puzzle of the two names. Here, as I see it, we have a choice of two possibilities. One is that "Hippolytus" and "Hippolyta" were simply the titles of the male and female attendants of the early Artemis. This, while the simpler hypothesis, seems to me the less likely. An alternative is to suppose that Hippolyta was herself a goddess, that either the name was one epithet of the mother-goddess (then or later known also as Artemis) or that Hippolyta was a minor goddess of the earth-mother type, later absorbed by Artemis. There is ample evidence that such local goddesses were frequently identified with Artemis.[16] Sometimes the old name would linger on as a special title bestowed upon her. Occasionally the Artemis of a particular place would be worshiped with an unusual rite, peculiar to one community and undoubtedly deriving from the cult of the usurped deity. The myths which tell of the various nymphs attendant on Artemis, stories often most inappropriate to a goddess of chastity, may in part echo the half-forgotten origin of the goddess herself; they may equally well be tales once told of the lesser divinities she has replaced. If Hippolyta was indeed one of these Artemis equivalents, we may think that the greater goddess gradually took over Hippolyta's place in the minds of her worshipers, just as easily and naturally as Euripides' Hippolytus allowed Artemis' image to substitute for the ideal of his dead mother.

Scholars have already suggested that Hippolytus originally

figures of myth where names are simply taken as given. If there is any etymological connection between the name and the myth, I suspect it is to be found in the detail, probably added last, as to just how Hippolytus' death was accomplished. And here I believe that the name came first. The bull as a means of destroying Hippolytus is natural because of its connection with Poseidon, Theseus' father. The horses are not necessary since the bull could have killed Hippolytus by direct attack. It is possible that the horses were added because of the already familiar name of the hero.

[16]For a short but excellent discussion of this problem, see W. K. C. Guthrie, *The Greeks and Their Gods* (Boston: Beacon Press, 1955), pp. 99-106.

bore to Artemis the relation which Adonis had to Aphrodite.[17]
I should suggest that an even more exact parallel might be found
in the relation of Attis to Kybele. We know that "Attis" was
the name applied in the myth to Kybele's lover and that he
emasculated himself in the course of a madness sent on him by
Kybele, who was angered by Attis' infidelity. The name was
applied also to the priest, who at the height of religious ecstasy
castrated himself and hence became an "Attis"—or, if one prefers, became Attis himself by a process of mystic identification.
A further step has been pointed out by Willoughby. "The newly
consecrated priest was thought of as a male counterpart of the
goddess. Hence he was sometimes called *Kubebos* [a masculine
equivalent for Kybele, whose name appeared also in the form
Kubebe]. By the fact of emasculation he had assimilated himself to the nature of the goddess. As an indication of this transformation he henceforth wore feminine dress and allowed his
hair to grow long."[18]

Admittedly Willoughby is describing customs of a much later
period. Nevertheless Kybele is generally accepted as being a
fairly pure form of the ancient earth-mother deity. It seems to
me (particularly if we accept Persson's ring evidence) that it
would not be going too far if we said that a goddess known as
Hippolyta had had a priest-attendant who, becoming her masculine counterpart, took on a masculine form of her name. In doing
so he was identifying himself also with a divine consort of the
type usually associated with the pre-Greek vegetation goddesses.
Possibly in the beginning the goddess was served by an actual
eunuch who, as time softened the myth, became a priest or worshiper merely bound by a vow of chastity.

---

[17]See in particular D. W. Lucas, "Hippolytus," *Classical Quarterly,* XL (1946),
65-69.

[18]Harold R. Willoughby, *Pagan Regeneration. A Study of Mystery Initiations
in the Graeco-Roman World* (Chicago: University of Chicago Press, 1929), p.
127.

The rest of Hippolytus' story would appear to support this view. If we are to say that originally he was a consort of a primitive goddess, then immediately he takes his place with other "year-gods," all of whom represented the annual cycle of vegetation. As the year itself grows from infancy to full maturity and then declines to make way for the new year, so the year-god grows to adulthood, makes fertile and thus renews the creative powers of the earth goddess, then dies (often is torn apart), and is later resurrected.

The similarity of Hippolytus' story to that of the year-god was pointed out as early as 1912 by Jane Harrison and Gilbert Murray, who, however, limited their discussion to the account of Hippolytus' struggle with Theseus, his death, and his later restoration to life. Jane Harrison points out that the custom of offering locks of hair to a local hero or year-god daimon is a common one and reflects one of the many *rites de passage,* an initiation ceremony to mark the transition from virginity to virility—or as here from maidenhood to the status of matron.[19] Such locks of hair were frequently dedicated to Artemis; sometimes the hero received them for the goddess.[20] There is nothing strange in this, since the hero and the primitive goddess' consort were doubtless at the start one and the same.

Even granting the validity of the argument up to this point, we have still before us the question of how the story known to Euripides could have developed. Certainly the human story of unrequited love and vengeance had taken form long before he wrote his tragedy. On the one side, we have a fertility goddess, possibly once called Hippolyta, and a priest-consort who for her sake actually or ritualistically sacrificed his virility, was killed, and was later brought to life again. In the later version we have

---

[19]Jane Harrison, *Themis. A Study of the Social Origins of Greek Religion* (Cambridge: Cambridge University Press, 1912), pp. 336-339.

[20]See Farnell, *op. cit.,* p. 66.

a young man who is devoted to a goddess now representing chastity and who rebuffs a mortal woman serving more or less as the incarnation of the fertility goddess. We also have Theseus.

Obviously no hypothesis offered to bridge this gap can be more than a reasonable guess. At best it will be good enough not to be actually contradicted by existing evidence. But recognizing that the theory is hypothesis only, I should say that the myth must have developed somewhat as follows:

First of all, Artemis when Hippolytus was first connected with her must have been a fertility goddess, who was responsible for his death as suggested above. Then as the character of Artemis on mainland Greece changed, two conflicting traditions remained. One said that Hippolytus was the priest or devotee of Artemis, the other that he was destroyed by the mother-goddess of fertility, who now could be only Aphrodite. The fifth-century form of the myth actually preserves and reconciles both traditions. He remains the victim of the fertility goddess, and he is still almost a masculine counterpart of the goddess Artemis and has, so to speak, ritualistically consecrated to her his virility by his vow of chastity. But this new form of the myth needs a different sort of motivation; once Hippolytus' chastity is explained as dependent on a goddess of viriginity, his function as year-god and divine consort is inappropriate. The solution is obvious. One always knew that the goddess of fertility was responsible somehow for his death. It must of course have been Aphrodite who killed him out of jealousy because of his extreme devotion to Artemis. Since in Greece Aphrodite apparently replaced Artemis as a fertility goddess, there must at one time have been some rivalry of the two cults, which would lend support to the idea of a conflict between the two goddesses even before the two could be seen as representing opposing abstractions. As for the later resurrection of Hippolytus, there would have been no reason for Aphrodite to accomplish this. Hence the act was ascribed to Artemis as it always had been, simply dressed up a bit in the later story by having Artemis appeal to Asclepius, who would be more reasonably expected to have the requisite power.

Up to this point the myth is hardly distinguishable from dozens of other tales in which the jealous Greek gods destroy one another's beloved mortals, and it could not have offered much challenge or opportunity to Euripides. It is the human instruments which enrich the story, and the problem remains as to how Theseus and Phaedra ever got into the narrative.

Theseus' entry is not hard to explain. There are countless myths echoing the historical replacement of one deity by another—witness the many accounts of Zeus' love affairs in which he apparently married or at least united with local goddesses, often becoming the father of a hero or heroine to whom another father was already accredited. [21] Helen is one example of these offspring; Heracles is a still better one since even his mother Alcmene thought it was her husband Amphitryon and not Zeus who caused her to conceive Heracles. I have already suggested that Hippolyta may have served as an earlier goddess so much like Artemis that she was absorbed by the latter with no conflict. It is probable that as Artemis developed and changed character, Hippolyta gradually became a shadowy figure but still lived on in people's minds as in some sense different from the great goddess Artemis herself. The similarity of names would continue to connect her with Hippolytus even though his function as priest-consort would be now associated with Artemis. It is possible that even before the arrival of Theseus, Hippolytus had begun to be thought of as the son of the earlier form of mother-goddess; but I am inclined to doubt this since there has never at any time been any suggestion of another father for the young

---

[21] In this connection it matters little, I think, whether we adopt the theory that Theseus was originally a god or that he was a legendary folk hero. In either case he certainly was associated with local figures of myth who were at some time worshiped; e. g., Helen and Ariadne.

man. In any case, if we grant Hippolyta the status of local
goddess, then Theseus' affair with her parallels a multitude
of other myths. The only other change effected by the later
myth would be that Hippolyta would be made the leader and
queen of the Amazons rather than a goddess served by them.

If we prefer the other hypothesis—that Hippolyta was not a
goddess but merely one of Artemis' Amazon-priestesses—then
the story of her relation with Theseus can be taken almost literally. The only difference between the myth as given in the
fifth century and my interpretation of what happened is the
question as to whether the Amazons invaded Attica from Asia
Minor or were already in the Peloponnesus, as I believe the
Mycenae ring indicates. If this view of Hippolyta is taken, then
Hippolytus becomes her son at the same time that she is made
Theseus' lover. I am inclined to believe that it is at this com-
paratively later date that the mother-son relation grew up,
whichever thesis we adopt.

I believe that we are forced to admit that Hippolytus was in
Troezen as local hero and priest-consort before Theseus began
to be worshiped—if indeed he ever was worshiped at an early
date.[22] The evidence as to the actual time and origin of Theseus
is entirely inconclusive, but certainly the myths are unanimous
in representing him as the opponent of the matriarchal societies.
He is almost killed by Medea but brings about her downfall
instead. Both Ariadne and Phaedra are carried off after hostile

---

[22]In saying that Hippolytus was established at Troezen before Theseus, I do
not necessarily mean that he was there before the Greeks. The name, of course,
is Greek. There are two alternatives. Either the Greeks found a goddess and
consort whose name could easily be twisted or translated into something Greek.
Or early Greeks, influenced by the non-Greek inhabitants, were worshiping
gods of their own invention in a non-Greek fashion. There is no real difficulty
here, and there are parallels. For example, the Olympian god whose name is
indisputably Greek—Hermes—is almost certainly to be identified with a pre-
Greek deity, represented or at least worshiped in the form of a heap of stones.
Cf. Guthrie, *op. cit.,* pp. 87-94.)

expeditions to Crete. Hippolyta is overcome in battle. Even Helen was kidnapped in her youth by Theseus. I believe that the act of making Theseus the conqueror and lover of Hippolyta and the father of Hippolytus is simply a way of saying that the Athenian sacred hero attached to himself legends associated with local figures. The statement that Theseus not only fathered but utimately was the direct cause of the death of Hippolytus continues—without really changing—the older story and underlines the conflict between the two heroes. Pausanias' report that the people of Troezen refused to accept the story of Hippolytus' being destroyed by horses may of course reflect merely local pride; perhaps, however, it may support the idea that the Theseus account has replaced an earlier version in which Hippolytus' death was accomplished without the presence of the Athenian king, a death which was but a prelude to triumphant resurrection and a token of his divinity.

What of Phaedra? Other writers have suggested an easy way out here. It is generally agreed that she was a Cretan equivalent to the earlier Artemis and/or the Aphrodite of all periods. If so, she functions for the goddess herself. It is still the fertility deity who is responsible for Hippolytus' destruction. I suspect that Phaedra became connected with the Hippolytus episode at the same time that Theseus did: that is, after Artemis' nature had been split and her worshiper's death ascribed to Aphrodite. If so, then Phaedra serves to link the two stories— the belief that Aphrodite was responsible for Hippolytus' death and the tradition of Theseus' conflict with him. Theseus killed Hippolytus but was impelled by Aphrodite. Phaedra, who is almost the mortal incarnation of Aphrodite, had already been made Theseus' wife. Thus in one sense she has usurped Hippolyta's place (as Aphrodite did Artemis') and through Theseus she destroys Hippolytus.

———

I should not for one moment wish to maintain that Euripides had all of this antiquarian research in mind when he wrote *Hippolytus*. In fact the most interesting observation we might make may well be to point to the startling transformation which the character of Hippolytus has undergone and the thorough humanization to which the myth has been subjected, chiefly before Euripides, but in all probability partly at the dramatist's own hand. From one point of view it is quite true that the question of the origin and primitive significance of the myth has no bearing on the play itself or on our interpretation of it. Yet it is possible that the story as it was handed down may have carried with it overtones and connotations of its original source. Although Euripides' Artemis shows no trace of the old fertility goddess, there is a suggestion of mysticism and religious ecstasy in Hippolytus' worship of her which is normally found only in connection with her Asiatic counterpart.

There is one small point which is of particular interest even though we cannot prove that from Euripides' point of view it is not pure coincidence. In the beginning of the play when Hippolytus offers the wreath to Artemis, he prays to her in words filled with obvious sexual symbolism. Under the guise of describing the meadow from which the flowers come, he praises purity and his own chaste life.

> Lady, this woven crown I bring for thee,
> of flowers I gathered in a meadowland
> where neither shepherd dare pasture his flocks
> nor ploughshare ever came, but in the spring
> *the bee alone explores the virgin field.*
> Virtue itself maintains a garden there
> with dews from running streams. Those men alone
> who have not training but a natural gift
> for temperance in all things equally
> may gather there what evil men may not.

The emphasis on temperance (*sophrosyne*), which we know Hippolytus to have interpreted as sexual abstinence, is significant. The figure of the plough in the field was a common Greek sexual metaphor. But most suggestive is the line

the bee alone explores the virgin field.

We may recall that on the Mycenaean ring, along with the three priests in women's clothing, was the bee. It is in part on the basis of this ring that I have offered the hypothesis that Hippolytus was originally a priestly attendant and consort to the early fertility goddess.

The wheel has come full circle.

DONALD SUTHERLAND, Professor of Classics at the University of Colorado, is a graduate of Princeton University, receiving his A.B. in 1936 and his Ph.D. in 1939. Since 1951 he has contributed reviews, translations, and articles to the *New Republic, Western Humanities Review, Kenyon Review, Yale French Studies, The Nation,* and other periodicals. He is the author of *Gertrude Stein: A Biography of Her Work* (1951) and the preface to *Stanzas in Meditation* by Gertrude Stein (1956). His translation of *Lysistrata* appeared in 1959.

HAZEL E. BARNES, Professor of Classics at the University of Colorado, holds an A.B. from Wilson College and a Ph.D. from Yale, and has done post-doctoral work at Columbia University and the University of Hawaii. Before coming to Colorado, Miss Barnes held teaching posts at the Woman's College of the University of North Carolina; Pierce College, an American college for Greek students near Athens; the University of Toledo; and Ohio State University. She has contributed articles and reviews to a number of scholarly and literary publications, is the translator of Sartre's *Being and Nothingness* (1956), and *Search for a Method* (1963), and the author of THE LITERATURE OF POSSIBILITY: A STUDY IN HUMANISTIC EXISTENTIALISM (1959), published by the University of Nebraska Press. A paperbound edition, with an Afterword, was published under the title HUMANISTIC EXISTENTIALISM in 1962.